In Between the Raindrops

By

Gilli-ann Prevett

Angela
May you days
be fun & free to
be you.
Gilli-ann Prevett

Published by Peregrini Press, a division of Awen Collaborative Limited

For inquiries related to this book please email: info@peregrinipress.com

Contents

FORWARD

I have thought for many decades my tale should be out there for people to read, but I knew it was too painful to record. That was until one night, just as I was drifting off to sleep, I sat up in bed with a jerk and heard myself say, 'I am going to write my story in free verse' and call it 'In Between the Rain Drops'. It sounds too good to be true, but true it is, this book was meant to be!

One year later and it's complete! I am so grateful for all the words that came to me at just the right time.

In between these pages there is the magic of story and just may be enough to change yours. Years come and go and the stories we tell ourselves can either stay the same or we can think something different.

My story is full of threads you may recognise in your own. Unpick them and be enlightened - even transformed. Understanding releases us into the truth, enabling us to dispel the myths we may have inadvertently created to fill the holes of hazy memories.

May you laugh, be in awe, sigh and sometimes cry your way through this book, knowing we are connecting on a deeper level.

THE NEW ME

I have been known
By many names
In my life time
Gillian, Gilly, Franky, Gill,
Darling and Gorgeous
At school I was teased -
Gilli Jones bag of bones

When I left my old life
10 years ago now
I needed a totally
Different sounding name
I wanted to get my ex's voice
Completely out of my head
I gave it a lot of thought

I was called Gill or Gorgeous
Originally Gillian
Now I am called Gilli-ann
I only added a hyphen and an n
I also changed the pronunciation
Of my surname
It now sounds French
It's my favourite name ever

Like my name I have become
A very different person
Hard won but so worth it
It has taken 10 years
But has seemed at times
More like 100

IN THE BEGINNING

Here I stand
Well no, I am actually sat
Surrounded by books
All calling my name
In chorus!
Reminds me of the times
When my children
Both wanted my attention
                    At the same moment
And 'mummy' became
The dreaded word
                    And sometimes I wanted
                    To change my name to
                    daddy

Why books now?

Giving you an insight
Into the many parts of my mind
Allowing you to get an
Understanding of my character
Interests and values
Where I am heading

I am a bookworm
But often inhabit
Many books at the same time
There is always
Another one round the corner
To many for one lifetime
So much pleasure

My mind always wanting
More, more, more!!!

BOOK ONE
Swifts and Us by Sarah Gibson

Swifts have been
Called angels (I am an Angel fan)
They sleep on the wing
One eye open
Half their brain awake
Finding warm thermals
High in the sky in
Communal dormitories
They can drift for 6 miles

They only touch land
When they nest
Mate for life, live apart
When not raising their young
They have been in our skies
Fifty million years

I'm in awe and wonder
Full of admiration
I fall in love with them
Their story feels beyond
Even my imagination
Like a fairytale
How did they evolve

Life is full of unanswered questions

BOOK TWO
The Body keeps the Score by Bessel Van der Kolk

Deeply complex
All about the mind and body
And the transformation of trauma
Giving more understanding
Of the self
Steering me away
From automatic habitual reactions
Opening up new options
Showing possible freedoms
Increasing self awareness
Asking questions
Finding answers
Breath, chanting, movement
Major keys to recovery

For decades
I have searched
For better ways to think
Looking for more understanding
Of myself and others

BOOK THREE
The Black Flamingo by Dean Atta

This third book
Written in free verse

It opens my eyes
In more ways than one
I learn new perspectives
An introduction to
Modern relationships
Acceptance seems the key

This book is filled with
Poems and pictures
Intermingled with story
Artist and poet
United as one
What a gift to me
I feel so excited

What follows days later
A light bulb moment
Called
In Between the Raindrops

BOOK FOUR
The Art of Encaustic Painting by Joanne Mattera.

Always looking for
New ways to paint
Colours and subjects
I saw this medium on
YouTube
So I bought the book

Three paintings later
All self portraits
I was able to incorporate
My love of collage
My interest in family history
And my fascination with storytelling

Perry Barr
10.7.10
My dear Em

Symbolic Self

I have wanted to make a self-portrait for years and at last it's here full of symbolism.

Starting at the top, a picture of ice that formed on top of my red car. I feel I've been trying to break through the ice in search of who I am all my life, and at last I'm getting there.

The blue writing in the background, found in my mother's belongings 36 years ago, is a love letter from my grandfather to my granny in 1910. The second letter from my other grandfather's brother in 1965 wanting to get to know me. I was 21 then and with none of my family interested in me I didn't respond, I so regret that now I really needed support and love but didn't understand it could be available.

The peacock's feathers are also a feminine form and a sign of the enjoyment I get from dressing well, the eye saying I can see you! My daily meditations enable me to see others more clearly, so seeing and being seen are important to me.

The leaf in my hair is a sign of fragility, the gold makes it special.

The knotted necklace, a ligature representing the stranglehold fear has had on me since I was 5 .... abandoned.

The bamboo is a sign of my strength. It's hard to stop it growing no matter what, which I'm so grateful for.

The beetle, though not a Dung beetle, we'll pretend it is. Placed here to eat all the shit I have had to put up with, from the men that were in my life.

I've always seen myself as a butterfly with its delicate fragility and the ability to fly. I have a need to be and feel free.

ARTIST

I am 10 years old
The most beautiful girl
In all of my class
Maybe the whole world
Has a three tier metal tin
It is mesmerising
For weeks I can't think of anything
Else
The tin is full of colours
Like rainbow sticks
I didn't know there were so many

This is my first experience of colour
Like being born with
New eyes
I want those colours
More than I have ever
Wanted anything

Julie seems to have
Everything I want
Beauty, popularity, brains
And colours beyond imagination
I wonder why
One person has it all!

I never get them
I forget them
When you can't have something
There is no option
My artistic ability
Doesn't get discovered
The light goes out

**
I glance out of my window
I can see a field and trees
I call it my field
And I am right
It is mine to see each day
Right now it's spring
And filled with forget me nots
To one corner bluebells
Bright lime green leaves
Drip from the trees
I have always loved colour
**

I guess when a child
Excels in one subject
The teachers
Don't feel the need
To see if you are good
In what was
And probably still is
Considered a lesser gift

I was considered
The maths wizard
The do everyone's
Homework girl

I find maths exciting
It fascinates me
How all the numbers
Slot together so naturally

This was a world
That made sense
A world I felt safe in
A world that couldn't lie
It remained constant

I was noticed here
Actually seen, praised
Was of value
Could do
What many others couldn't
I excelled
And apparently just this
Gave me a good future
Full of possibilities

Sadly at 14
My education came to an abrupt
END

What you don't use
I have learned
Over the years
You sadly lose
The neural pathways
In the brain shrink
Thankfully others can grow

Now when I think of school
My first thought is
Sticky current buns
Every school day
Crates of cold milk would arrive
Wooden trays full of buns
One of each with my name on it
The milk tricked down my
Dry throat
With the penny bun
Filling my stomach
Giving me energy

The best use of a penny
Ever
Each day it gave me
So much pleasure

As I close my eyes now
In my mind I can see
So clearly as if yesterday
The plump brown shiny top
Toasted black currants
I can taste the sweet spice
Feel my sticky fingers
Lick them in my mind
Magically a smile appears
Memories so powerful

To this day I love sticky buns
Only now they need
To be gluten free

At 29

A small flicker of moonshine
Sends me off to art classes
I need a good reason
To escape domesticity

I haven't drawn since school
Have never painted
I haven't a clue
What to do or how

The result a landscape
I don't need to draw
Clumsily painted
But enjoyed immensely

Did I hope to find
A talented artist inside me
I don't remember
If I did I was disappointed
VERY

Wow 47 already!

Son goes to University
I cry buckets
Thought I would never stop
Half my world gone
His life now
Not ours
I know it's right
But it leaves a gaping hole
I grieve his loss

Daughter in sixth form
Very independent
Not home much now
Has her own life
Intelligent, modest and distant

What can I do now?
I'd given my life to them
All of it
When I am not a mother
Who am I?

**

Remembering this now
I can still feel in my body
That deep sense of loss
Mothers all around the globe
Will I know understand this
Seldom talked about
But so deeply felt
**

WHO AM I

The Sun streams through
The kitchen window
I go outside
Watching the breeze
Blowing the shadows of grass
White daisies
Yellow dandelions
Grey on the pavement
Dark shadows
Matching the grey in my heart
I sigh

I seem to sigh
For months
Stuck in my self-pity
Heart so heavy
It's like I'm pulling
A weighted trolley behind me

Grieving the loss
Of my children
20 years
Of togetherness
What's left
Collected tears
Filling bottles

Time passes
As only time can
One moment at a time
One day at a time
Each week follows the next
And the months hang together
In clusters

I hear on the radio
Schools short of pupils
Someone in England
Age 30 ish
Took up a place
I THINK!!!!!!

I continue to think
I am artistic I know
Knit my own sweaters
Redesign the patterns too
Make dried flower arrangements
Grow some of the flowers
Collect wood from the beach
Buy a glue gun, oasis, wire
Spend weeks making

House full of mess
Time-consuming
And exacting
Nerves frayed
Like Rumpelstiltskin
I spin growth
Into gold
For my children each year
At Christmas

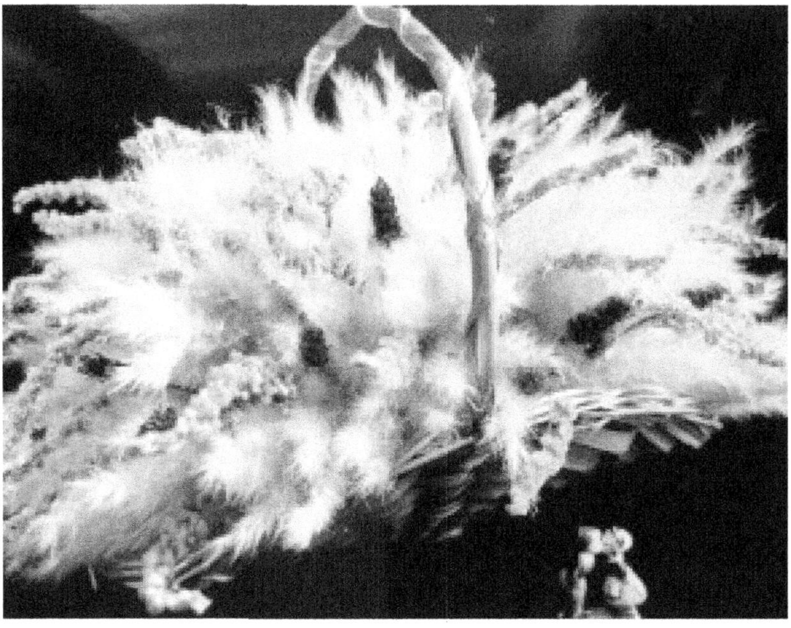

I AM STILL THINKING

I know how to make pottery
Had private lessons once

I am good at Floristry
I have a keen eye

It all goes around in my mind
I'm trying to work it out

Eventually I go to the local
Comprehensive
Tell the teachers what I've heard
Ask if they can help
Give me a place
Doing A-level art

They get back to me
With an encouraging yes

What fun
I'm part of a group
Of teenagers!!
Get a feel for them
How they tick
Make friends
One in particular
A whole new world

I don't quite know
What I was thinking
Perhaps
I pictured myself making pots
Or knitting, sewing
I didn't expect what came next

They want me to draw!
I don't know that one
Pencil and paper
I'm useless
Where do I start?
I dabble with paint
Read some art history
Feel an idiot

I can't draw
I try and fail
Over and over
Nothing changes

Then the teacher says
You have to start
Really looking
Not drawing
What's in your head
But what you SEE

**

Thinking backwards
I was courageous
But so naive
Following my dreams
Pushing my boundaries
Filled with new hope
It feels like a miracle
As if it was someone else
Not little old me
**

It's summer holidays
I have spent a whole year
In my A level class
Escaping from drawing
But I can't do it any longer

I sit at my dinning table
Looking
Drawing
Trainers, flowers, hands
Anything
For weeks, that's all I do

Holiday has ended
I now understand
The process of drawing
But that's only a start

To draw you have
To practice a lot
Like learning the piano
To be really good
It's practice, practice
Practice

Painting and drawing
Become a thrill
Well the painting does anyway

Yet still I haven't
Rekindle the passion
Glimpsed
When I was 10
Three tier
Rainbow pencils
They're still forgotten
For my A-level
I make a model of

Claude Monet's wife
Using papier-mâché for her
Face head and hands
Fingers are the hardest

Then a big hat
Made of cardboard
With dried flowers around
                    The bonnet
Ones grown in my own garden
My favourite part
A real piece of my life
For so many years

There is an open book
Monet's wife Camille's diary
Made of clay
With writing on it
A poem
I still have this
On the table in my hallway

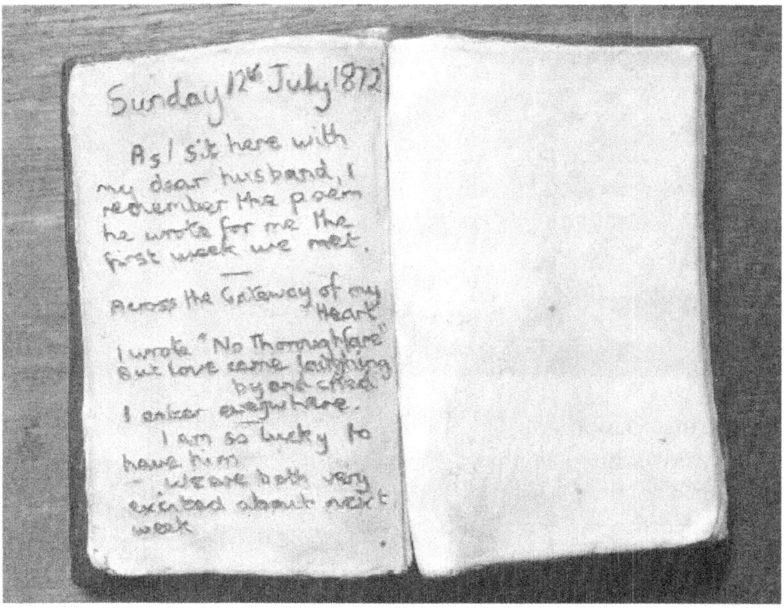

My final exam piece
Painted in oils on canvas board
I learn so much
As I paint this
I am thrilled with the result
Expect to get a high grade

The dissertation - oh
I haven't written anything
I mean anything
For decades
During this process
I discover I am dyslexic
Now that surprises me
It also explains a lot

(5 year diary started in 1957, recently discovered, written for only three and a half months and you can clearly see I am dyslexic)

I have no confidence
Just know I can't
Write a dissertation
My boyfriend helps me

What I don't realise
He is just showing off
Doesn't really care
If I pass or fail

And

I don't question
His abilities or knowledge
But most of all
                    His honesty
Drags my results
                    Right down
I could have written it
                    Easily on my own
Just needed someone
To believe in ME
So I could believe in myself

I get married again
Move up north
It seemed such
A good idea at the time
I loved him so much

Help bring up his children
They are just 8 and 11
Love them like my own

It's so hard though
I'm given no control
So don't get respected

They grow
Such a nasty childhood habit :-)
As all kids do
They go off to boarding school
Their grandmother insists

I start art classes
Near to a university
I want to feed
The restless artist
Inside of me bursting to be seen

By now I am quite
A good basic artist
Self taught mostly

I hear the university
Close by take mature students
So I apply
I'm accepted ….wow!
The University of Central England
It now has a different name
Located near Cadbury's

With young people again
What a treat for me
They are so full of life

I'm computer illiterate
Knowing absolutely nothing
Never used a computer
Or a mobile phone

Makes it hard for me
It is another world
Thankfully I am better
At painting than most

My first experience
Of any university
And I love it

We are given projects
I start making a picture
Out of sweet papers
Bin Laden is newsworthy
My theme is terrorism

All waste bins in public
Areas like stations
Cease to exist
So sweet papers
End up on the floor

I am partnered with
A very young student
She sadly doesn't follow
The given brief
And surprisingly quickly
Told to leave being
Unsuitable for the course

I don't get a mark
For this project
Because they mark as a pair
Don't even give me any feedback
I am pretty cross

The tutors teach you to think
Outside of the box
These days I don't
Even think of a box
There is no such thing

I START

It's like finding new corners
In the recesses of my mind
I am so excited
I create a display
A platform covered
                    In black velvet
On top I place an ice cube
Wrapped in a metal cage

I film it as the ice melts
I call it 'icecapology'

I so love the thinking
For once my mind
Is put to good use

It is fun and freeing
Interesting, challenging
I can see why
I was born with this brain
At last I am not bored

Then

So sorry ha ha ha
I take pictures
Of my husband
As an ice cube
Melts in his mouth
Catch his expressions
He could be moody
                    Even without the
Ice cubes
You grab the opportunities
                    When you can
A bit of sadistic
                    Revenge
Another form of escaping

Next

I filmed an ice cube
Dripping into a candle
Of course, it was 'snuffed out'
'Iceasphyxiated'

Now

I blew up a very small
Polly bad
Stuck the tip to a wall
Told them it was
'Floating ice'
They said
There was no ice in it
No I said it 'Icescaped'
Another show
Of 'icecapology'

**

My observation
We don't stop playing
Because we grow old
We seem to grow old
Because we stop playing
**

Art History

Exams on art history

I remembered by heart
The notes I had taken
In the lectures week after week
But getting the right books
Out of the library

Without understanding

The high technology
Seemed impossible
Very few staff to help

It is like another world
One I can't access
No matter how hard I try
It is a huge disability
I've not taken
A written exam since school
I tell you I am scared

I couldn't write
Not one single word
I just froze! Mind a total blank

Once I had started
I was away
Answering the questions
I had learned by heart
Not ones from the library
I couldn't answer those
But the others I got right
And I passed the exam
I was so excited

I thought carefully
About the next project
Eventually I chose
To look backwards

Found photos of my childhood
I had so many
Thought about nursery rhymes
And incorporated the two

It helped me to see clearly
Just how cruel my
Young years had been
Gave me more understanding
Bought my authentic feelings
To the surface
I was able to see
New truths
Ones I hadn't acknowledge
Even after much
Counselling
There was again
Still more pain to heal
More anger to be released

I went on to grieve
The childhood I never had
Was able to understand
Just a little more

It is a very slow process
Layers of pain so deep
If it all came out at once
You wouldn't be able to handle it

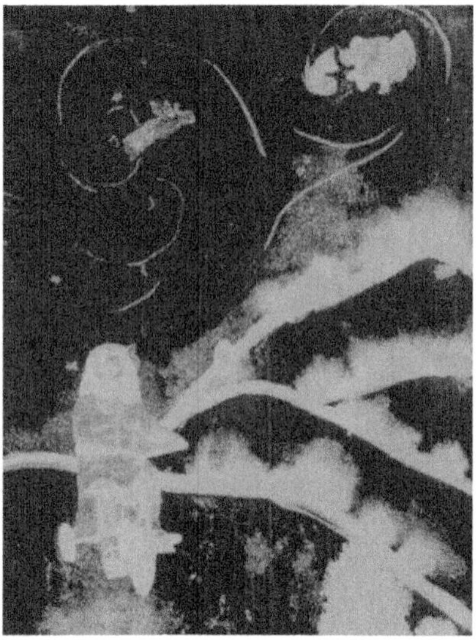

My tutors loved the work

I wanted to show
My father this work
To share these pictures
Showing from my perspective
How my young life had felt

Once again I was told
This time by my husband
That my dad was much too old
It seems he was
TOO old at 60 and 70
Now too old at 80 90 and 100
I never got to say
How unloved I felt
Never got to share
Vent my feelings
Of neglect and abandonment

NOW and my father

He is gone
I never told him
Never challenged his actions
How his decisions his choices
Made for my young life
Had left me with deep
Mental scars
Sometimes still visible
A life time later
Ingrained in every cell
Of my body
So they tell me now

My father in his 90's
Tells me as a child
He never felt loved
So the seed of unlove
Gets handed down
But the buck stopped here
My children are loved
So very deeply

I asked my father
To relate his story
He was now 97
Just 3 years before he died

He dictated it orderly
In chronological order
Without any emotions
Just one fact after another

This enabled me
To see how emotionally
Unavailable he really was
And gave me more understanding
He wasn't just like it
With me perhaps!!!

I wrote the story
Word for word
Well almost!

At first he asks me
Why would I want to know
About his life
It had been terrible

This is coming from a man
Who has declared
How happily married he is
Has been for some 60 years
4 children with his second wife

In so many ways
A wonderful life
A few big hiccups
As with all of us
                He is a maths teacher
                And preacher
Gentle man
                When not angered
Still, in his 90's
                Thinks he has a temper
                But with no understanding
                That he has a choice
                To allow it or not
His childhood is still
                At this point in time
                Imprinted on his mind
Marriage to my mother
                Was traumatic
And it doesn't seem to have
                Been healed
By his 60 happier years

Our negative thoughts
Play such a strong part
In our lives
So much easier to remember
Than the positive ones

The hurts get lodged, stuck
Because they are focused on
And deeply felt

The good times
Don't need resolution
They come and go
Where as our unresolved pain
Stays with us
It haunts us to the grave
If we don't deal with it

The Choice

Layers of waves roll, as if on pogo sticks
Water, being obedient to the moon's pull
Patches of foam, changing every moment
Pleasing my eyes, now my pain needs to dull

As the moon is in control of this sea
So my frustration, seems in control of me
Need to ride the waves, not be the waves
Where has my anchor, my deep core gone?

Fierce tigress, roaring like thunder
Anger, of a million unseen soldiers
Fighting my reality, breathing short
Waging war against myself, and others

Sitting right here in warring mode, again
This part of me mostly hidden from view
But now, claws are sharpened and ready
Riding on the back of my righteous ego

Mind, spiralling in its negative circles
Same words repeated over and over
With heart racing and missing some beats
Feet tapping, hands shaking, eyes twitching

War sits side by side with my soft one
Each of them wanting all my attention
Both with a very different agenda, but
Equally determined to get their own way

Halt, stand still, take a breath, and another
Time to review all my possible options
Breath calms me right down, red mist, it clears!
She floats in slowly, her light ready to steer

As soft liquid gold, she flows like the sea
Always sat patiently, awaiting my call
Perceptive, tender, gentle, loving and wise
She's my ally, friend, she has my size

Bending my will, to align with some peace
Listening to her wisdom, watching my tongue
Realisation dawns, war had me fooled
Feeling soft plucking at my heartstrings

Using the waves to wash away my anger
Reflecting its energy, deep down inside
Watching how I am forever changing
My perspective starts to alter its course

Acceptance is at the root of the answer
Whatever comes, it's not personal, I know
It has something to teach me, that I 'm sure
Surrendered, I connect to infinite self

When soft comes, she lights up the whole room
War, shrinks into the corner quite soon
But he knows an ill wind will come along
And the battle will commence once more

It is now September 2017
My father has celebrated
100 years "Happy Birthday'
A party and letter from
The Queen

His physical health
Is a real challenge
But his mind
Is as sharp as a pin
On the other hand
His wife
Has the onset of dementia

So between them
They have one body
And one mind
Which enables them to manage
Once again

They complement each other
My father has a fall……
He has been ill
A number of times
Over the years

I have been to say
My farewell
First time 10 years ago
When he was in hospital

We've had a number of calls
Warnings of his
Imminent demise
So by this time
For me he feels immortal
Like everlasting flowers,
They go on for ever,
Or
You think they will

I am aimlessly strolling
Around my local charity shop
I love a bargain
I have felt depressed
For many days
So need an outing

I see this statue
I love it's form but it's
More than that………

One problem it's very dirty
I don't know if it'll come clean
I also wonder if it will
Keep reminding me
Of my sadness
I decide not to buy it
It has other ideas
I seem unable to
Walk out of the shop
There was such a pull on me
It felt greater than just physical
There seemed a spiritual
Happening

At this point I've no idea
That my father is about to die

That same night
My brother called me
Father had taken
A turn for the worst

He said he might not
Pull through this time…..
I knew definitely he wouldn't

I start to clean my statue
Something to do that would
Allow me to process the news
I scrubbed it with a toothbrush and
Washing up liquid
It stayed dirty

Next I got a scourer to it
It still didn't clean up

Then I started to howl
As I realized my father
Was in the process of dying
Without ever being the father
I so needed him to be
The next day
My brother rings
As I knew he would
Father has passed away
My daddy has gone too
I went back to the statue
It was so strange
As I wiped it with another cloth
It gradually became clean
As if my tears had cleansed it

She is so beautiful now
All week I have had her close
Found in her great comfort
I feel she is me

A representation of my life
I see her grief and beauty
Allow her to grieve for me
It's like I know I will always
Be grieving the loss of a father

But I can allow her to do
Some of the grieving
So I can have some relief
She will always be by my side
Sat to the right of my TV
I often look at her

My father confirms
He isn't after all immortal!!!
The funeral comes along
My daughter and I go together
My son arrives to support us too

He hasn't spoken to my father
Since he became an adult
I had to respect his actions and his pain
He couldn't bear to be a part
Of a man's life - one who had
Caused his mother so much
PAIN
He was asked to be a coffin bearer
That was very touching for me
He couldn't reconcile to his grandfather in life
But in death, this was so fitting

As I sit writing this I am in tears
I rarely cry….due to my antidepressants
Looking back on happenings
One can often see more clearly

Sat now in the family funeral car
We are following the hearse
The funeral director walks ahead
Dressed in black with hat in hand
Held against her chest
A black stick in the other she marches
Slowly and solemnly showing respect
It moves me deeply, the image stays

At the crematorium we watch….
As the coffin comes in I see
Not the coffin though it's there
I see my fathers broken body
Broken as I have been much of my life

He is now at peace gone to join
The spirits that have gone before him
They will show him the way
Will he be reunited with my mum
In death are we all united in love
My intention is to let go of him
He has played his life's role
Some of it good, some of it mmm….
We only get one turn of the wheel

For me

It's now time to live more in the light

BACK WITH ARTIST

I get a year at college
Then my husband decides
It's time to move on
Goodbye to my education
ONCE AGAIN

Before we go
A new gallery opens up
I hear about it
As it is close by
They are offering
A greatly reduce rate
As they are not known yet
I give it a go

It's very exciting
A lot of work
But I have a gofer
Strong husband
15 years my junior

All my paintings
Hanging on these
Beautiful vast white walls
The exhibition space
'It's all mine'

The paintings look amazing
The space gives them a
Great sense of grandeur
They don't feel like mine
It is magical

My 11 year old dream
Has become a reality

Sue one of my teachers
Had an exhibition in Cardiff
As we are walking
Down the stairs
In St David's Hall
I say to her
'one day I will have my own
Exhibition'

I'm not sure if at that time
I believed it was possible
But it is always good
To have a dream

Opening day arrives
A preview with drinks
My family gather
This really is all about me

To my surprise
Agents arrive wanting to sell
And promote my work
I hadn't thought of that

My husband says he will
Make all the arrangements
With these fellows
I am in a daze
People are seeing ME
And it feels good

I sell ten of my paintings
And wait to see
What happens with the agents
I wait and I wait and I wait
Keep asking my husband
'Have you heard from them'

They never did get back
It's years till the penny
Drops in my lap
I now know he discouraged
The agents sent them away
Didn't want me
To be distracted from my job
Of looking after his every need

This book of verse
'In between the raindrops'
As I write it
I find I can't always
Dodge the drops

Every now and then
In fact often it would seem
There is a splash
A few drops, a few tears
Even a downpour

Life so intricately
Interwoven like
The scrambled eggs
On my breakfast plate today
You can't separate
The white from the yoke
But
I am trying to use an umbrella
As often as I can

We move down south
To a church at war
An internal power struggle
Dysfunctional parishioners
All wanting 'their way'
It is hugely challenging

Playing my part
Like an actress
On a stage she didn't choose
Calming and encouraging husband

Sharing my story
Including my depression
To help these people
Share their challenges
Encouraging openness
And hopefully helping
To form a bond of love
Being the antidote to war

Children growing up
Teenagers now….never easy
I feel pulled from pillar to post
Feeding everyone's needs
Except my own
Cajoled by my husband
Into teaching
Art to a parishioner
Two very long years
Someone with no eye
For colour or for form
Teaching acrylic and oils
It was soul destroying

Eventually ignoring protests
I release myself
Find a watercolourist
Teacher that inspires

I watch fascinated
As she keeps mixing
Colours often on a dirty palette
Stops them being too bright
She says

We use salt, bleach, cling film
We learn so much
Gaining confidence again
Feeling so FREE
At last this artist is happy

And guess what
I found the rainbow colours
My ten year old remembers

I get my own studio
Space just for me
My painting ability blossoms
Life moves forward

The trajectory changes
My umbrella breaks
Even blows away
Thunder and lightning
Rain reigns!!
Continuous for more than a year
I leave my cruel husband

I GO BACK HOME 2013

This broken artist
Lands in my old
                    Stomping ground
With a thud
What's left of her

Escaped my controller
The big bully boy
With his constant little threats
Put you downs and demands
Once again I ask the question
Who am I
If not a wife or vicar's wife

But not right now
I need all the help
I can get from
My family and friends
To find some peace

I need to feel loved
                    And respected again
Honoured and believed
Seen as a person with feelings
Shown some care
Heard and understood

None of my clothes fit
But slowly I put on some weight
I'd lost three stone

While I'm trying to get well
My Ex goes and marries again
I feel so sorry for her
I try to warn the church
And send her leaflets
Where she can get help
                    And find refuge
If she ever needs to!

Slowly, gently determined

I put one foot in front
The other follows
I will find my feet

Now my hands need to create
No art materials with me
Everything left behind

I start to rip up newspaper
Looking for words
Colours and shapes
Buy PVA glue
Make my new hosts
A very modern picture

I remember the old bible
My friend Maureen gave me
It was on her shelf
She said this one
Wasn't used she had others

It's nearly Christmas
I have little money
So start wrapping
Words from the bible
Around stones I've collected

Making sure the messages
I want to give, stay
On top so they are seen

My homemade paperweights
Jesus's story and teachings
A real Christmas connection
Presents for helpers
People who have blessed me

The theme flows on
I start using the bible
As collage on pictures
Words of expression
Giving life meaning
All come together

Feeding my needs

As I move from
One life to another
It's a huge change
Parish life was so busy
Full of people and happenings

Now on my own
I do what I want to do
When and how I want to
This is good
There's no one controlling me
But
It's a challenge
Not one I would choose

**

I have small fruit flies
My only company these days
They follow me around
Even go upstairs with me
I am so grateful to them….life
**

THE CROSSING

The Crossing was
The first picture
In this series
8 years ago now

Using my very active mind
Words and pictures
Gave it some joy
A reason to go on and live
Revealing my inner world

With no one to talk to
Except the canvas
Right in front of me
We hold the space
Together
One idea leads to another
I give birth
Eventually to triplets :-)

KILLERS

Words from the book of Daniel
He was saved by God
In the lions den
Guess how this
Came into my mind?!

It was my son
Who saved me
From the roaring Lion
That was my husband

The whole of this picture
Is a play on words
Their meanings and symbols
Asking questions
About life death and salvation

WHOSE POWER IS IT?

The weather this year
Winds are ferocious
Mighty waves crashing
God's powerful nature
Inspires my artist

With joined up thinking
I go to Ecclesiastes
Find a newspaper cutting
Of the storms

Next I see the binary code
In another paper
Man's power
Which makes me ask
Whose power is it
Doesn't everything come
From God

These two excerpts
Form a great structure

I love God's words
So full of wisdom
They are so profound
They get me thinking
Deeply…..so deeply

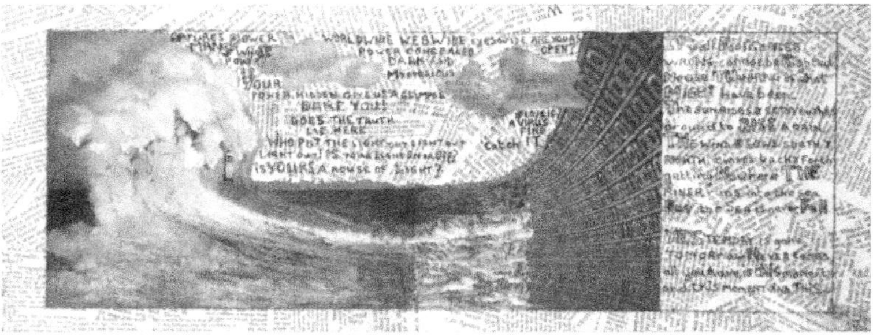

All of these works
On recycled canvases
Bought in local
Charity shops
Like my new found clothes
As I arrived with very little

Life moves on
I seem to say this a lot
We know not what's coming

Change and adapt
That's what we all need
Leaving the past behind
Looking to a new future

Learning to be grateful
For what we have
Acceptance
Seems the big key

I join the local art group
First night I go
I'm given newspaper
So nothing new here
Along with thin PVA

It's the time of the
Scottish referendum
The news is saturated
Feels like there is nothing else
It starts to drive you crazy

I rip the newspaper
And what emerges
Surprises and pleases me
It turns into flags waving
Angry faces everywhere
Later I add Words
From the radio
Dotted over the newspapers

Made so quickly
Not premeditated
This is how art's
Meant to be
I feel invigorated

I am beginning
To learn it's the process
Not the need to
Produce a finished piece

It's the doing
That brings the joy
I am awakening
Little by little

NO THANKS
HEART

This next painting
WE WILL REMEMBER
Our nation is paying homage
To all those
Who gave their lives
For the greater good
Individuals each one of them
War, mans feeble attempt
For more and more power

My painting is to honour
Every person from all countries
Blessed souls gone to rest
Before their time
I am a pacifist
So really feel the needless pain
Of those killed in fighting

This picture has once again
A bible background
Words taken from those
Passages read at services
Of remembrance

The sky is made
From a hospital gown

The music on acetate
Is the last post

Men's hats from all sides
Thrown at the cross
Which symbolizes home

The poppy was already
On the recycled canvas
Then there's the unknown soldier
Representing all soldiers

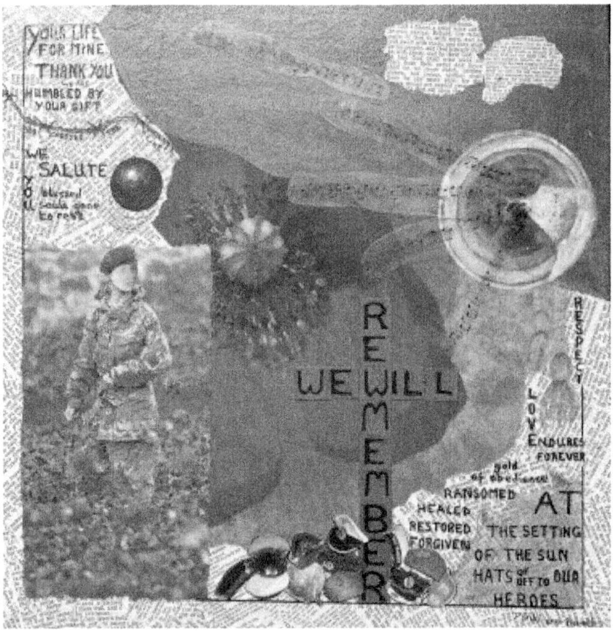

We Will Remember

Your life for mine, I thank you
I am humbled by your gift
I salute you blessed souls
Gone to rest before your time
Love never dies, it lingers on
In the hearts of those left behind

We will remember all who died
No matter what nationality
Showing through this very action
The futility of war, man's sin
Let's prize peace and contentment
Death then may wait for aged men

Yes at the setting of the sun
We hear the bugler play again
The 'Last Post', a somber note
A sign of respect for all souls
Ransomed, healed, restored, forgiven
May we be all pardoned too

Let us not try to justify
The act of war

So very very slowly
This fragmented vessel
Repairs it's broken pieces
And as in Japan
The cracks get filled
With GOLD

Words of comfort
Encouraging myself
Changing the negative
Habitual phrases

Hush don't rush
Becomes a very important
Phrase not to be forgotten

I am building
Something that will last
I dearly hope

Life or Lifeless

My life like bowl
Half full of magic
Light as a feather
Sky top and rooted

My non-life's bowl
Half empty of nothing
Chipped and broken
Needs to be fixed

Along comes my circle
Writing friends and more
Word teasers pleasers
Plucking tales from the air

Joy mixed with love
Peace in the making
With hope interwoven
Pure gold is spun

My so sad half bowl
Made better than new
Cracks filled with gold
A celebration of words

More life's cracks to fill
Thank goodness

I like to feel
Part of something
Bigger than myself

As an artist
You spend a lot of time
On your own
I quite like my own space
But still need connections

Being an artist
It's such a precious gift
You get to have fun
Be inspired often daily

BUT

As artists have found
Down the centuries
It's not an easy life

You have to be famous
Before people want
To purchase your work
You can only get known
By selling your work

So you get stuck
It feels as if
No matter how accomplished
You become
It's very hard
To make ends meet

Selling your work
Feels like a constant
Uphill struggle

Artists, I know many
Get depressed, feel dejected
With houses and studios
Full of work they can't sell

I only charge £10 an hour
For my work
But it takes 20 - sometimes 60
Hours to paint
That's without
The thinking time

I watch on YouTube
As famous auction houses
Encourage people to bid
There are some lovely works

Then I see some others
Selling for thousands
And I know it is only
The name being sold
Not how good the work is

We as artist watch
People like Tracey Emin
Doing often ordinary work
And
If our names were on it
It wouldn't sell
But hers sell like hotcakes

What makes me think
In this vein started
About six years ago

I went to the
RA Summer Show
Yes in London:-)

It was such a thrill
I so looked forward to it
I saw a lot of special work
Names I knew some I didn't
It was a great experience

Also there
We're a lot of ordinary
Not really very different
Pieces of work

I thought my work
Would out shine these
So the next year
I enter 2 pictures
You saw them earlier
Called
Killers and The Crossing

They were both rejected
£25 to enter each one

I was disappointed
Not one to give up easily
I decide they will
Go to the ball
As Cinderella did
Not left in the ashes
Or on my wall never seen

So I get them printed
Not an canvas
But on two t/shirts
One my size and one
To fit my son

We go to the show

Wear our T/shirts
And my son takes
A photo of me
Guess where?
In front of Tracey Emin's work

The nearest I may get
To being famous

ADVENTURER

EARLY 60's

My two aunties
Living in Birmingham
Courageously move
To Cornwall's coast

Betty and Harold
Buy a small hill top
Shop and caravan
With mobile catering

A large van with side opening
Along with contract to supply
Soldiers at the near by fort
When in residence

Mary and Arthur move
To Eddystone cafe
Right on the beach
At bottom of a cliff
With no roadway

All supplies are winched
Down the cliff face
The place only has gas
It is all very basic
But it's breathtakingly beautiful

The first few years
Go well for them
In the summer
Such a delight
Especially for daughters
When they reach dating age

Renowned for it's surfing
Long sandy beaches
Boys come in their droves

I once shared a canoe
With one of the boys
Sharks came close by
"Just basking' I'm told
They won't hurt you

Exhilarating scary stuff
Could over turn the boat
Now they tell me
I'm frightened of the water!!

What memories
What a place
I had almost forgotten

Sitting here now
My face glowing
My mood shifts
To one of joy

I can smell the sea
Hear the pop of seaweed
Feel the sun warm
On my well oiled skin

Boys still a mystery
That's not really changed
Recall handsome eyes
Smooth deep voices
With a Cornish drawl

Tanned skin dripping
With saltwater as they emerge
Muscles pumped
From canoeing and surfing

I was in love with Jim
My cousin wanted him
And this was her territory
I was warned to 'keep off'
Neither of us get him
He stays single

All of his life
I wonder if he was meant for me
Feels like such a waste
He was such a lovely person
Deep and meaningful

Uncle's a fisherman
We eat it fresh from the sea

One day with nets
Buckets in fact anything
We could get our hands on
We ladle out sprats
In their hundreds
And thousands

Oh were they tasty
Milky sweetness
With homemade bread
Heady days

But the sea gets rougher
Waves engulf the cafe
Breaking the windows
Everything sodden
Terrified they flee

The sea so powerful
It topples the heavy tray rack
In the middle of the kitchen

Each winter now
They have to evacuate
Leaving their home
To the elements
Never being sure
Just what damage

Nature will do

I can't imagine how that
Must have felt

Each spring means refurbishing
Re-evaluating their situation
Till one year they leave
They can't sell it
They lose everything
Not sure about insurance

Out of interest I look online
I am wondering if the cafe
Is still a building

Or

Has it been washed away by the sea
What a huge surprise
Eddystone cafe
Up for sale May 2022
With large extension

A Million pounds
I get a tour of it
Online it's amazing
So different to then

Outside it looks much the same
In the same spot
Right on the beach

I wonder if the sellers
Tell a story that's honest
Or will the new owners
Get destroyed
By the crashing seas
And have to wave goodbye
To their home
Like Aunty and Uncle did

I feel very curious
As to if....Aunty and Uncle
Were deceived
When they bought their beautiful dream

What a magical place
So full of mystery

EUROPE WITH GEORGE

Secretary needed
To travel to Europe
My boyfriend says
I volunteer
George is great fun

Jewish by origin
He makes guitars
Sells the strings too
I've never been abroad

I'm fascinated
We go to many countries
Stay in posh hotels
Sometimes
Shabby ones another
He says he likes to surprise me
And boy does it work

My biggest discovery
Continental Quilts
No heavy blankets
I will never forget
The difference just this
Makes to my life

Down floats over
And all around me
Touching me with
                    A million soft gentle kisses
My favourite kind
Like drifting on clouds
I'm in heaven
Well almost!

His selling goes so well
It's my note taking
I tell him, we laugh…..

EMIGRATION 4TH APRIL 1968

Months of form filling
I save hard for my flight
A return ticket
Just in case
Joining my friend Joy
In down town Toronto

New York here I come
The night I land
Yes that very night
Martin Luther King
Murdered!!!!

I hear it on TV
I'm so shocked
Sitting on my bed
In this huge Hotel
All by myself

The people here
Love my accent
So ready to please me

In the lobby
I dropped my bag
It spills everywhere

This so handsome man
'Can I help you mam'
With a beautiful smile

Smells expensive too
Helps me to collect myself
Picks up all my small things
Tampax and all
Doesn't seem to notice
My embarrassment

I appear to be different here
Popular, noticed and heard
It feels so good
Until I eyeball
A policemen with a gun
I shudder and feel vulnerable

I gather it's meant
To do the reverse
Should make me feel safe
Give me reassurance
But I'm not convinced

My second day
I head for the
Empire State Building
Up to the 86th floor

Though afraid of heights
Five lifts I think it was
I had to do it
Because that's what you did
In those days….I think

I walk to the edge
Of the open air promenade
Camera in hand

You can apparently
See sixty states from here
I point my camera
Click my finger
Hoping I have caught something
Then race for the elevators
I'm done and have proof!

It makes a good story

Would I do it again
No I would go find
A good coffee shop

Or look for some green space
I got wiser :-)

I head for the station
Get the train going to Toronto
800 odd miles
A long tiring tedious journey

But it has it's moments
We stop for breakfast
I try remembering what I had
I know it looked so tasty
Maybe cinnamon buns
That's why it's hard to recall
They were not homemade :-(

I'm staying with friends
From my childhood
Joy, Mac and Mary
In an apartment building
With a swimming pool
Very posh and modern
Ahead of it's time

Gill I say
This is your new home
At last I have a base
That won't disappear

I have not been here
More than a week
I'm told they are leaving
Going back to the UK

They say I need to find
Somewhere to live
I am gobsmacked
Deeply deeply hurt
They invited me here
'Come to Toronto'

My flight 3 months away

I search and eventually
Move into a house with
5 boys and another girl
I share her room

Finding work……..huge challenge!
No recognised qualifications
I end up in an office
Typing insurance policies

Throughout my life
I've made a point
Of never saying I'm bored
BUT
And I'm on the 12th floor
Frightened of heights

I am so miserable

I left my interesting job
In London for this!
Working for Granada TV
My safe lodgings
With my friend Jean
And her lovely parents

**

Going out to the pub here
You have to queue for a seat
Once sat
You can't carry your drinks
To join other people
It's hard to make new friends
**

Mary - Joy's daughter
Invites me to the
30,000 islands
Her boyfriend Don
Has a marina there

I get my very own
Boat with a motor
It's beauty - breath-taking
There's water everywhere

I'm staying on an island
With raccoons close by
They can open doors

I'm told there were bears here
Never saw one
But I imagined them!
Definitely a scary thought

The trees are so tall
The sky disappears
There's a small river flowing
Threading it's way through
This wild unpredictable land
One night Dan invites me
To go fishing
With just a torch and bucket

It's black, maybe even blacker
He teases me
About bears behind trees
Well, that is what I hope he is doing

The torch lights
A narrow path for us
We find the river
Sure enough there are
Many fish swimming by

He stoops over and
Shines the bright light
Into the flowing water
One of them is dazed
It can't take it's eyes off the light
He says they are called sucker fish
Don't know if he's joking

He scoops it up
It only just fits in the bucket
Must be fourteen inches
That's just a guess

It thrashes about
Then we hear a crackle
Could it be a bear?

Phew it's a raccoon
I take in a deep breath

We head for home
Put the fish in the bath
Say goodnight and thanks

Mary gets up for a wee
In the early hours
I hear a scream

Much much later
I find out
No bears inhabit this island

It's a kind of magic
Riding my motorboat
Anywhere I want
The sense of freedom

Was awesome
Never felt so adventuress
Before or since
There is a young man maybe 16
I'm 23 YEARS OLD
He fancy"s me
Story of my life
Always the young ones
I felt it would be crazy
To take him seriously

I have always needed
My relationships
To have a future promise
And the principle was right
Could he have been
'The one'?

5th June still 1968
We hear on TV
Robert Kennedy
Has just been shot!!
There is total disbelief
Surrounding me on all sides

What is happening
I just want to go home

Before I do, a must apparently
We go visit Niagara Falls

What a magnificent sight
It takes my breath away
Though I am not sure
If it's the view or my fear
Probably a bit of both

We make the deep descent
Into this huge tunnel
Which travels under the falls

The ROAR that meets us
Is overwhelming, deafening
My adrenaline so high
I just want to run away

Am I glad I made the trip?
At the time definitely not
But looking back
Just seeing the falls
In my minds eye
I can omit the noise
Yes it was an awesome sight
God's almighty power

RETURN TO NEW YORK

I meet up with Robert
A friend of a friend
He has a small basement
It was hot, I mean HOT
He was so lovely
A real gentleman
Gave up his bed
Slept on a wooden bench
For ME

He guided me to
The Central Park with a
Statue of Hans Christian Anderson
I fell in love

Next we went to the
United Nations Monument
The wall of words
From the book of Isaiah
'Let us beat swords into ploughshares'

It so moves my heart
With a 9' tall statue
Donated by the USSR
The Sculptor was Vuchetich
Historical times these
Russia and America
Reading from the same page

We head for Staten Island
Traveling by ferry boat
Past the Statue of Liberty
It is huge
This feels so surreal
All those times seen on film
And now I am here

We paddle on the sea shore
So cooling and fun
I love to feel the sea
On my feet sand between toes
It brings back childhood memories

A very special time
(I feel privileged when I look back)

But I am now homeless
Going back to what?
All my friends now scattered
I am totally alone

I mean completely alone, no family
My father didn't want me
To even know where he was
With his new lady

My mother too ill
I can't handle her
I have no money
Only a large suitcase

The day after I land
My left big toe
Balloons bright red
Doctor tells me I have gout

I feel lost and forlorn
I don't have any roots
So I put a pin on a map
It takes me to Cardiff
Where do I start
I buy a newspaper
Girls looking for flatmate

17TH JULY 1971

I get married to Jeff

We honeymoon
2 weeks in Corfu
There are very few hotels here
Uncommercial and raw
In many ways

Beautiful beaches
Gentle lapping waves
Warm enough to swim
Though I am nervous
Water frightens me

Hermit crabs
Everywhere you look
I've moved house
To this point 25 times
What a palaver
Often months of work

But the crab
Just waits
Along comes a shell
Eyes it up for size
In minutes - a new home

That's the way to do it
I watch them for hours
Not a lot going on here

We hire a scooter
License not needed
'Licensed to kill'!

I sat on the back feeling safe
Until we go up a hill fast
I shoot off backwards
With no helmet or hat
It wasn't provided
What a lucky break
I only had grazes

We roam for miles
Reach out to far away places
Strange to remember

Old ladies all dressed in black
I wonder if they
Hand down the clothes
From generation to generation
I ask myself how old
Do you need to be
To dress all in black

Found a local cafe
With fresh fishy food
Real Greek cooking
Not like the hotel
With their strange meat
Which I thought might be horse

It's HOT
Only in New York
Have I been hotter

My husband hurts his foot
Another bad mood
Couldn't dance with me
Before the injury
So fat chance now
But Tony Blackburn
Asks for a dance
Jealousy increases the mood

We walk to the petrol station
Most nights
Nothing else to do
Greek music and dancing
Around petrol pumps
Strange when you look back

Everything you hope for
From a honeymoon
Doesn't happen

**

As I write this
Jeff is at my daughter's
Dying of lung cancer
I know I should feel something
But I feel nothing
**

I try hard to please
Show him I care
Offer understanding and love
But he makes no effort in return
No tender moments
I feel unappreciated – flat

This is the template
For my marriage
16 years of trying to
Fill the hole of his absence

On the plus side
One boy - genius, gentle and caring
One girl - gifted, loving and caring
I am so grateful
For these beautiful
Little people who
Completely trusted me
Teachers of love
We grow each other
Always there
Me, them and us
Tiny connections
Interwoven with love
The strongest yarn

Weaving a tapestry of life
They complete me
My first works of art
Love so deep
So high, so wide
Like atomic waste
Indestructible

I am so proud
To have birthed
These two precious beings
My gifts to the world

3 MONTHS SABBATICAL

September 11th 2001 (9.11)

With my second husband
Traveling to Italy
Through Switzerland
Car bursting with supplies
3 months into the unknown
We feel like pioneers
We're looking for different
Expressions of
Spirit over the centuries
On the border
Stopping for the night
Monday 10th September
Comfortable we sleep
Rise for breakfast
Which was a veritable feast
Cooked meats and cheese
Lovely bread fruit juice

We walk to get a newspaper
One of our habits for years
The atmosphere feels tense
We don't speak German

Walking past the shops
We see a television
Seems to be showing a war film
Keeps repeating the same scene
Over and over again
People are aghast!
We don't find a paper
They had nothing in English

We head back to the hotel
Put on the television
We can't understand
What's happening
All morning we are confused

Try ringing home
No one answers
Something is very wrong
Is the best we come up with

Our big question now
Do we continue our journey
How safe are we
Are our families at risk

We decide to wait
Keep looking for
An English newspaper
It takes us days
We carry on our journey
My fingers wanting to cross
But we place it in Gods hands

Eventually we connect to home
News is still sparse
But we get the gist
The whole world changed
Everywhere is different
Unsettling and threatening
People suspicious and jumpy

We arrive at our
Countryside flat for a month
Wonderful it's overlooking
Vineyards, peaches and sweetcorn
I pinch myself

We swim in the sea nearby
It's full of seaweed....yuk

Mosquitoes feast on us
Even with mosi nets
And anti midge lotion
We spend the days scratching
But it"s always worse at nights
A month Later

We head for Gaeta
Booked months in advance
Not realising it's a naval base

Our residence is used
As an overflow
Dormitory for the military
It's often noisy
People coming in late
Leaving very early

The roof is a large sitting space
With chairs
Which overlooks the sea
Also the Naval base

Being tourists
Our cameras are always at hand
We shoot from every angle
Memories for us
Pictures to show friends

We go exploring
Find ourselves
On top of a strange hill
Take pictures as you do
Some men turn us around
Waving their hands at us

Later we learned
The sign we couldn't understand
Said No Entry
In Italian of course
We head back to our base

Days later
Returning from Rome
There's police at the reception
Asking for English guests
Receptionist sends them
To our neighbours
Who are English

But she knows we are Welsh
So they can't want us

They took our neighbours
In for questioning
About reports of people
Taking photos on Naval property
Also of the Naval base

Oh poor them
It was obviously
Us they were after!

It seems we had
A narrow escape
Like an espionage movie
9.11 made everyone nervous

In the sitting space
I get out
My first canvas
The blank white space
Stares back at me
For days we stay blank

On finding an art exhibition
Just up the road from us
I fall in love
With a painting of Jesus
The eyes talk to me
I wonder if I should buy it
Only room for one souvenir each

Back with my canvas
I try painting Jesus
Background looks good
Dry it on the balcony

While eating dinner
I hear a crash… bang
On looking up
See my painting has fallen
Down to the roadway below

I dash down the stairs
Just in time
To see a large lorry
Riding over the canvas
It's broken beyond repair

I decide to go and buy Jesus
With the sparkling eyes
But it's gone, sold
BOO hoo
But not surprised
I still to this day regret
Not buying it straight away

ROME

Only in distant dreams
Dare I even imagine
Visiting the Vatican
So when offered the chance
I jump at it
I ask my husband 'in jest'
Will we see the Pope
He won't be showing
I'm told

Tickets in hand
We enter this world of
Majestic splendour
Floors, walls and even ceilings
In your face beauty
Room after room

For three whole hours
We walk and view
Eyes on stalks
Murals so…. vast
With immense detail
Michelangelo
Just one of the famous names

So quiet in here
As if loud voices
Would damage these relics

Guards watching and waiting
I imagine their lives
Every day just standing
Waiting for excitement
That never comes

This place is crammed
With priceless ancient art
Murals, sculptures, pottery
Paintings, architecture and more

7 kilometres of art galleries
Span this region
Endless priceless wealth

I start this day
With great expectations
A chance of a lifetime
One of the privileged few
My mood is high
The sun is hot
Not a cloud in sight
Even indoors
I know this is true

BUT

Just as the sun
Goes down on earth's beauty
So to my mood sinks
With each passing hour
I become more numbed
Too much to see
It all starts to dull
The shine disappears

Like a glutton must feel
Sick in my stomach

How many ordinary people
Put their meagre earnings
In collection plates
Though they go hungry

They are encouraged to give
With promises of salvation
Answers to their prayers
A place in heaven

Peasants struggle
Church gets fat
Power for Men
But not for God

He asks for humility
And a contrite heart
A faith in Him
Love for each other

Jesus said to us
Do as I do
He goes amongst His people
Serving them
Giving not taking
Asking only
Faith in his Father

Father forgive them
They know not what they do

My husband's mission
For his 3 month sabbatical
Studying past miracles
Shrines and churches
Hearing the many stories

We see
Saints heads
Centuries old
Skin without decay
A finger untouched
By the passage of time

Revered and worshiped
Though not admitted

I personally end up with
More questions than answers
Seeing the human condition
Exposed and so needy

I'm asking the question
'Is what we have viewed
Contrived or real'

Is the church corrupt
Should it be bringing attention
To these relics
Raising false hopes
As it collects the money

Or

Does the church provide
Psychological support
Giving people something
To hold on to
Hope for the hopeless
In this life of uncertainty
So full of turmoil

As I grow older
The scope of my understanding grows
So often I see
The foolishness of mankind
But that of course
Has to include me

Being the observer
Is what makes the difference
Riding the waves
Not being the waves

I still fall into the sea
Floundering with the mass
But I am becoming
A more experienced surfer

SAINT FRANCIS OF ASSISI

All churches by now
Are beginning to look alike
But there is one!
With a very different atmosphere

Many centuries old
It still has a living presence
A monastic life
On our way in
We pass some of the monks
Dressed in their 'habits'

In the lower chamber
Which is a vast space
There is a tangible presence
As if you can touch
Those spirits gone before

There are daily prayers
Holding this space
Connecting the generations
Over the centuries

Walls soaked in prayer
Maybe imprinted
By spiritual vibration
Breath of a billion
Chants, hymns, devotions….
So permeable, so real
A spiritual soup
You can feel at one with

At last God at home
With His people

Many years later in fact 21
I close my eyes
And I can still feel it
The wonderful experience
Of souls dancing together
Recognising each other's presence
Immersed in God's Spirit

SICILY

Next on our list to see
A very long journey
Italian motorways
So many under repair
Or construction
Often no sign of workmen
Just cones upon cones

Long bridges everywhere
So long
You can't see their end
It feels as if you will
Drive off them and into space
It's scary
My mind finds it hard
To come to terms with this

5 lane motorways
At Reggio Calabria
Little heed of the rules
Horns honking
Crazy meandering
It's pot luck we survive

Going over on the ferry
We hear tales of the Mafia
Sends shivers down my spine
Are we really safe
No way of knowing I guess

Off to Palermo
It's now mid November
Still piping hot
Unusual for this time of year
We are often told

Everywhere is deserted
Nothing is open
It's like a ghost town
We have a beach residence
Miles of sandy beaches

So picturesque
Mighty waves rolling
A thunderous sound
Greet our ears as we arrive

Humidity is very high
Our sheets feel damp
The walls inside moist
Night time is a challenge

Swimming too dangerous
Not what we expected
It read very differently
When choosing this place

Husband wants to see
Mount Etna
It's a very long journey
This is not for me
Recently erupted
Still burning hot under foot
Definitely not for me

On my own
In Mafia country
Can't stop feeling edgy
Distraction is needed

Start my second canvas
I am painting our beach
At sunset it's beautiful

We can walk for many miles
On this shoreline
Paddle out feet
When the sea is calmer

I start the memory in paint
Sketching it out first
Buildings in the background
Oil paints and brushes
I relax into it somewhat

Our base is a semi detached
With the owners next door
Who don't speak any English
But they smile a lot

Our waste water
Irrigates their small garden
Seems there's not much rain here
They grow a few veg

I close my eyes and imagine
Living here all year
In winter the wind blowing
Sea thundering
Two months in summer
Boiling hot and humid

So close to nature
Open to the elements
Real life connections
And believe me
Nature is really in charge here

Peoples lives on the same level
As the powerful sea
I see clearly now
Just how protected
I am and life is for me
Makes me feel like a sissy

I wondered if in winter
These people too have to move
The sea being on their doorstep
May be literally
It reminds me of
Aunty Mary's cafe
Off Eddystone lighthouse

My father buys this painting
His wife persuades him to
It hangs in their dining room
Which they use every day

When my father dies
Age one hundred
(He had told me he was ready
To die when he was 90)
But he doesn't want
To leave Pat on her own

Pat his wife now with dementia
Goes into a home
The house gets sold
The painting goes
To my brother
Life keeps moving on
Irrespective of how we feel

MOTHERHOOD

Time to give birth
And be born in unison
There is a bright blue sky
And the day is crisp
Like the first Cox's apple
I feel so full of expectation

I am being induced
Because my baby
Is just too comfortable
I know today's the day

It's a long wait
Giving birth it seems takes time
When I'm fully dilated
The induction machine
Just stops working

I am told I have to push
It will be harder than usual
Because I have no contractions
But I can do it ...they say

At this stage
I just want it over
So I do as I'm told
Push with all my might

I am too small for his head
So they make a cut
Slowly slowly then suddenly
This little being arrives
5.20 6th February 1973

They tell me it's a boy
Healthy 8lb 2oz and kicking
He is placed in my arms
A real baby so surreal
I look at him
He is still part of me
My heart and his heart
Bonded together forever

His presence is overwhelming
A feeling so powerful so strong

I know I will do anything
To protect and care for
This tiny creature of mine
The love flows to and fro
Weaving strands of togetherness

17 months fly bye
I know Nathaniel needs a friend
A sister or brother
To share the journey
I was an only child
Didn't want that for him

I was expecting within a month
It was a bold decision
I was not well last time

But this time
I am unable to keep
Any food down
I also get dehydrated
I have to stay in hospital

They suggest an abortion
Maybe it's nature's way
Of telling me somethings wrong
But I won't do that
As Meatloaf said
I'll do anything for love

April 10th
Mild for the time of year
My daughter is ready
100% know she's a girl
From the very beginning

She is in no hurry
So 30 hours later
We are both triumphant
12.20am she arrives
On 12th April 1975
Weighing in at 6lb 12oz

Tiny little fingers and toes
I can see them now
Tall for a girl
She is such a cutie
We fall in love

I feel more confident
Done this before

But I was so wrong
Two at a time
All by myself

We struggle together
She is constantly ill
I feel for her
She cries a lot
But we have each other
I've got you my girl
I'm here ready
To meet your every need

I am so blessed
Two beautiful children

JOURNALIST

Definition (occupation or one who keeps a journal)
When did I start
A distant memory
Like misty mornings
A few words here
Then some more
The mist clearing
As the words
Go on to do their healing

The rain of pain
Sends the pen to paper
The sun comes out
Pages stay blank

Winters can seem long
Summers far too short
Autumn filled with dread
As winter approaches

Spring sunshine
Sparkles on the deep
Waters of understanding

Fading into the distance
Bringing the present
Right into focus
Again the circle of life

Flowering and dying
Regrowth and renewal
What will be will be
With it the certainty
Of everlasting change

Sat here mid September
Sun still warmish
The waves rolling in
Rocks wet and glistening
I love a sea view
In recent years
More and more rocks

Installed by man's hands
Beach is unrecognizable
Access impossible now
For older people like myself
And for the very young
Sad and disappointing

But

I am sat here
Enjoying the sounds
Grateful for life
Knowing time to be
Doing what I enjoy
Is such a privilege

My journaling
Is in part responsible
For my much improved peace
My hand and mind
Joining together
Showing just what
Is inside my mind

It jabbers away
Has a will of it's own
Till I give it
All my attention

Reminding myself
I am not my thoughts
I have a choice
What I believe
Where to put my focus
How I frame my world

The view I choose
Finding the right perspective
That's what's important
This changes my emotions
Helps my journey
Enabling more peace

I've been through
So much in my life
Had way more than
My share of problems

Pain too deep
For most to experience
Or even imagine it's depth

Fear so great
And for good reason

Fear creating
Fear of fear itself
Ingrained habitual
Woven into every cell
Held in the psoas muscle
Sitting hidden in the hips
Holding on to the trauma

To experience a little
Of that which I've felt
Watch a horror movie
Then imagine living
With those feelings

Once for a whole year

I am strong it seems
I have survived
In the last years especially
Have also thrived

Writing is so wonderful

It finds ways
To reach parts of you
That nothing else can

An interlude of space
Time to stop doing
The ever constant
Lists of to-do's

You become aware
In between the thoughts
Rattling constantly by
There are treasures
Insights and wisdom
Waiting to be found

As I sit and watch
People coming and going
Wanting to see the beach
On a sunny day

I see they don't really know
Once they have sat
Watching the sea
From the rocks
What to do next
They are lost, fidgety
I get it, I've been there

When I come armed
With paper and pencil
The journey has a point
I am very content
Magic starts to happen
All on it's own

(I am smiling now)
As if another person
Is holding my pen
I am so grateful
For her love and time

Looking around me
I'm home now
Needing to write
As I am feeling low

I decide to
Count my journals
Not done this before
19 in all, wow!

I destroyed a lot last year
Ones filled with deep pain
I didn't need to revisit

There are still some old ones
Some devoted to art
Still more with notes
Lessons that I've taught
Meditations, art journaling
Mental health tools
New poems being birthed

Closing my eyes
I see in my mind
The galaxy birthing stars
Everything new has to be born

Bringing forth
New beginnings
Sewing of seeds
Germination and birth
Necessary and satisfying
God made us
In His own image
He the creator
Makes us creators too

Letters float around
In the recesses of our minds
A word forms
Flows into a sentence
Which stretches
Into a paragraph

Then page after page
A chapter comes forth
It doubles and quadruples
Eventually a book is born

With interaction it grows
In another's mind
Sparks new ideas
The work gets shared
Changes as it spreads

Seen from many perspectives
It becomes larger
Than the sum
Of its original words
An ever revolving
Evolving cycle of life

When I first discovered journaling
I would pour out
All of my pain
No particular order
Pages full of negativity
That was where I was
Angry, fearful and confused
But with little resolution

I didn't know how
Where would one start
To sort through
The years of neglect
Moving on to
The years of abuse

Like looking for the end
In a matted cotton reel
Or the beginning
I couldn't find either

Still carrying inside my heart
A large black mass of despair

The words in my head
Hammered like nails
Piercing my body and mind

I felt I knew
Jesus' pain on the cross
Except mine wasn't over
In a few hours or days
But through decades

**

As I sit
Drinking my tea
A drip escapes
Charging down my cup
Never quite reaching
It's goal
My lap, and my lovely
New cream jumper. Phew!
**

I got counselling
For many years
Poorly administered
Was I too much of a challenge
May be
Until one day
I found Ann

She starts the healing
With her knowledge
She is highly trained
And very experienced
Together we unwrap
The parcel of pain
Exploring my past

The one person
I can trust with my truth
We go deep
Mostly dealing
With distant issues

After years
We start to explore
My current problems
Within my marriage
But she betrays me
Starts working
For my husband and his team
No longer impartial
I find I can't trust her

**

I pause here
Look out of the window
I don't like this memory
I watch the wind
Moving the trees

I anchor myself
In the here and now
Watching the smoke
From a distant chimney

Imagine the cozy warmth
Of logs burning bright
The picture comforts me
**

I escape, leave
My abusive husband
Of 17 years
I was so broken

I had lost 3 stone
I couldn't eat
Could hardly swallow
Wasn't sleeping
I am found sat
Rocking in the corner

My son to the rescue
Takes me to a cottage
Cares for me
Let's me talk
The truth of what happened
Not the lies fed to him
By my cunning husband

7 years later
I find Christine
An amazing teacher
Counsellor psychologist

Slowly over the years
My life starts to change
I'm really listened to
She understands me

Gets who I am deep down
Encourages me

I work hard
Do all my homework
Am told she has never
Had anyone who works so hard

My attitude and perceptions
Confidence and understanding
Grow like yeast rising

I find secrets hidden
From me for so long….
I am intelligent
Emotionally and intellectually
At last I see some
Of my possible potential

**

I look outside
It is raining hard
But it doesn't matter
I have sunshine
Here in my heart
And I am so grateful
**

My journaling changes
Gradually over the years
Of self-reflection
CBT shifts my perspective
Teaches me to change
The patterns of my thinking
Gives me some control
Turning my negative thoughts
Into life giving ones

My heart, mind and spirit
Feel lighter BUT
My body still keeps
The score
It always will I think

I have to pace myself
Use the many
Emotional tools
I have learned
Over the years of
Climbing the mountains
So I can see
The view from the top

It is beautiful
Up here where
The air is fresh and clear
My arms fly open wide
As if I can fly

Now my journal
Is used for resolution
If something anything
Is upsetting me
Or I feel angry
Fearful, grieving, in pain
I go to my journal

It takes effort
Sometimes I can't be bothered
I find other things
I think I need to do
BUT in the end
If I carry these emotions
That I don't understand
I spiral into depression

Now a days
It's not for long
As I take cold showers
Each and everyday
Which has helped hugely

But

Eventually, I will stop
Get out my journal
Then wonder why
It took me so long

Why did I fight
Because deep down
I know from experience
That journaling
Will enlighten me
Lighten my load
Giving me understanding
Enabling me to find some peace

I find myself repeating
For myself as much as others
'It takes effort
All things worthwhile
Take effort'

Life is about choices
All the time, all the time
We are making choices
Some seemingly unimportant
Others monumental decisions
They all determine
Who we are and whom we will become and where

COUNSELLING

I think Americans
Have a better attitude
Counselling for everyone
Where there is
No shame

Here in the UK
We whisper our needs
Not wanting to be judged
As a bit bonkers

Personally I think
We would all benefit
From knowing ourselves
On a deeper level

Looking to break
The bad habits
Collected innocently
Over the years

Gaining understanding
Of our past experiences
To enable a better
FUTURE

**

I look around my lounge
Seeing all the autumn leaves
I've collected
All curled up on surfaces
Different shapes and sizes
Life comes and goes
Because they are sheltered
From the elements
They will look beautiful all winter
I know because I did it last year
**

Living with more peace
Connecting to love
Loving ourselves first
This then enabling
Us to share that love
With those around us

Giving us and the world
MORE HOPE

The Beatles had it right
'All you need is love'
It is the starting point
Of all good human connection

Tracking our minds
Is so vital
To good mental health
Finding the joy and peace

Not believing
All the lies
They feed us

Erkhart Tolle
Tells us
'Identification with thinking
Is the root of suffering'
And I see this as truth

This makes it so important
To keep tapping
Into our minds daily
Turning our negative thoughts
Around to positive
As CBT teaches us
We are what we think

I am so grateful
For all the teaching
I have received
Over the many years

My counsellors
Listeners and teachers
So willing
To share my pain

They undertake
This most challenging task
At what cost to themselves
I ask myself

Some of it so deep
Private and very personal
Their's being the only ears
To hear the workings
Of my mind on that level

Scary stuff

Helping me to find
Who I was born to be
Reframing my view
My inner and outer world

Such dedicated guides
Enabling me to find
The right pathway
And the best version of myself

I AM SO GRATEFUL

EMOTIONAL TOOL BOX

Like a physical tool box
Sometimes you
Grab something handy
Rather than search
For the right tool

The box grows
Becomes a shed
The shed becomes
A garage

Lost in amongst the mass
You can't easily find
The right tool

You know you must have one
But stopping long enough
To search doesn't happen
You just get on with your day
The problem remains unresolved

What I found I needed
Was a prompt
And some determination

Time given is always
Worth the effort
Because I find more peace
My body finds greater comfort
I feel a happier presence

It's the 'to do list'
That pressures me
Into thinking I haven't time

This seems like a good opportunity
To write out some
Of my more recently
Gained emotional tools
Not just for you the reader
But for myself

22 Enough sleep
23 Mindful eating
24 Mindful walking
25 Body scanning
26 Fill in CBT boxes
27 Allowing emotions
28 Recognising emotions
29 Be kind to yourself
30 change your story

My older tools
Still very relevant
So I am listing them
Not in any particular order

1 Deep breathing
2 Start the day with positive thoughts
replace any negative ones
3 Diet, hydrate, hygiene
4 Positive affirmations
5 Grounding yourself
6 Opposite touching
7 Press pause button
8 Comforting yourself, includes cuddly toys
9. Mothering yourself
10 journaling
11 Relaxation
12 Meditation
13 Being grateful
14 Acceptance
15 Balance, timing
16 Stop complaining
17 Art and crafts
18 Emotional socks
19 Play with inner child
20 Nurture inner child
21 Exercise

COUNSELLING SESSION

Haven't seen my counsellor
For five or six weeks

I get lost in doing
Forget my tools
It's autumn
With it comes sadness
Is it the dark
Or is it just me
Dreading the winter

My counsellor
Listens and talks
We revisit
My existing tools
Looking at ones
Already in my box
But from a slightly
Different perspective

I feel my resistance
Wanting to be more joyful
But at the same time
Needing my hurt
To be visible
Really felt and understood

I am feeling cornered
In lots of areas
Of my life right now

I talk about my experience

Doesn't matter
How many different
Dating sites I go on
How good my profile
Which I change often
What messages I send
If no one lives close by
Or no one messages me back

There is nothing
Absolutely NOTHING
I can do
To resolve my loneliness

It's the loneliness
It gets into everything

It seems however much
You enjoy what you do
If there is no one
To share on a daily basis
Your thoughts and feelings
You get to feel
EMPTY

Life can get to feel meaningless
Endless disconnection

People don't talk
About their loneliness
As if ashamed
1000's of us
All going around
With polite smiles
Feeding off
Our phones and the internet
Trying to find
Satisfying distractions
Connections that give us some love and life

I am enough
Is a favorite saying
From guides and teachers
But we were not made
To live alone
We yearn to belong

My counselling sessions
Always different
Talking about where I am
At that particular time

One of the conclusions
From this session
Was I am doing all I can right now
I need to be patient

MEDITATOR

For just over 10 years
Nearly every day
Missed maybe 5 a year
For 20 to 30 minutes
Between 2pm and 4pm
A well establish habit

Come rain or shine
I lie listening
To guided meditations

They come in many forms
With varying names
The aim is similar
To bring your mind
Into this moment
Then this moment….
Here and now
Letting go of fears
For the future
Or regrets of the past

Asking your mind
To notice what's
Happening right now

Concentrating on
Your breath or
Your body or
What you can hear or
What you sense or
See (if your out walking)

The only way
To grow your awareness
Is to practice, practice and practice
I seem to say this a lot

As I Sit (Meditations)

1.
I look for answers
Ways to chill my mind
And I remember
Just breathe, the first step

Now concentrating on NOW
Breathe in and slowly out
Feel the breath where it is
Nose, chest or tummy below

Breath, breathing it's self
No need for you to help
Mind wonders, that's ok
Just bring it back, feel the breath

2..
Another answer
Feel my feet on the floor
Body where it touches the chair
Weight bearing down and heavy

I find a comfy place in my body
Maybe hands, legs or feet
I explore and enjoy the feeling
I stay with it for as long as I choose

Mind wonders to past or future
I bring it gently back to my body
Grateful for the peace I'm getting
Being in the here and now

Why go to all this trouble???

The benefits are huge
Though not at first

It's a discipline
If you're like me
You like to be free
Do what you want

When and where
It goes against
The grain of your character
To have too much routine

But

I want change
Need more peace
And clearer vision

And

This is something
I am capable of
It cuts into my day
In return it gives life
Energy for later

Slowly very slowly
My mind accepts
Bit by bit
I become calmer
I start to enjoy
In fact look forward
To my created space
Though not always

Meditation alters
Your outlook
With clearer vision
You can become an
Observer of yourself
And then of others
When you choose to

You notice the small
What was
Once insignificant
Words and gestures
Reading in between the lines

It's scary sometimes
Seeing so clearly
What others don't notice

Sometimes it's things
You would rather not see
It feels too personal
Understanding others
Possible before they themselves

You want to help
But help needs
To be wanted and
To be asked for

I'm told and agree
There is a great
Universal awakening
Beginning right now
I feel privileged
To be a part of it

MINDFULNESS

So much more
Than just meditation
It's a way of life

We are all born mindful
As children we stay present
It's wonderful to watch
Then we start to worry
Different times
I guess for everyone
Depending on the circumstances

In my sixties
I meet mindfulness
For the first time
Too ill to read the rules
Being present
I am told is the answer

By people who
Have only read about it
In books they studied

10 years on
I am still learning
I get what to do
But to do it
Constantly
Seems impossible

However

I can be present
When out walking
Looking at nature
Listening to the birds
Standing by a stream
Smelling the air
Picking flowers
Concentrating on
My feet each step
They all take a turn

I had hoped
After reading
Elkhart Tolle's
'The power of now'
That presence would
Become very natural
A second nature
So to speak

My aim is to surrender
To the moment
Finding silent space
Inside my mind

This has happened
But only for short
Snapshots in time
When I remember
To be present
Bringing my mind
To here right now

Is it because
I started so late
In my life, I ask myself
I don't know many people
Who meditate
So I can't answer this

Just bee zz!

I have listened
Over these many years
To loads of excellent
Guides and teachers
I grow and change
And so do my
Meditations

I move on
Find new ones
As I progress my journey
Forever discovering
Different and deeper ways
Always evolving
Ready to accept change

With so much gratitude
Once again we're here

Insight Timer
My favorite App
At the moment
100's of teachers
Wise and experienced
From all walks of life
Around our world

My latest guide
Takes me on a wonderful journey

I am lying down
She guides my mind
Through the body
Connecting with each part
Then with the whole
Until eventually
I am just being

My body now feels
Like an expansive cloud
Floating in space
So still
I'm aware of awareness itself

I get excited

If I meet someone who meditates
It happens so rarely
It immediately feels
We are connected
At a deeper level

I so pray for the world
That more people
Will awaken to meditation
We would all benefit
Realising we are not a single wave
But part of an ocean

GRATITUDE

8 years ago now
I was given the name
Of a book
By my dear friend Olwen

It was a slow read
Beautifully poetic
Touched my own pain
As I read about hers

A sad joining of minds
Where her depression
Mixed intrinsically with mine
Often difficult to separate

This book changed my life
In big ways and small
It is called
'One thousand gifts'

Ann Voskamp
Challenged me
Time and time again

**
As I write this
I know I need
To read the book
Once again
Delve into the pages
To discover more
An up to date version of me
Will be looking
I have goose bumps
**

I have grown so much
Since the last time
Remembering snippets
Of how I felt then

I see myself now
All though through
A glass darkly
I am very different

Life was so challenging
I hated living alone
I had lost my old life
And I needed
To find a new one

I still loved
My husband
Hated him as well
Such a conflict
Mr Very Nice
Then Mr Extremely Nasty
Like two different people

The emotions
Tore me apart
I travelled down
Two different roadways
Sometimes even within
The same hour

**

I have just lit a candle
To bring in some light
This space started
To feel like thunder
Everything is better
With illumination
**

One of Ann's
Greatest challenges
To us the reader
'Write 1000 thank you's'

I take up the dare
Writing a few words each day
I still have this book

Revisit it occasionally

Gratitude slowly slowly
Filters into my life
I become more aware of
All that I still had
Started to appreciate
The small gifts
Seeing with new eyes
Life being made up of
Thousands
Of small intangible thoughts
Gestures
Smiles
Hopes
Dreams
Breaths in and out
Understandings
Love
Words
Praise
Thanks
Hearing
Listening
Seeing
Feeling
Touching
Inner gifts

You get the idea :-)

**

I look around me now
See my art hanging
On the walls all around

Photos of my family
Fill a big space
Thirty two of them
All this from little me
Rising from the ashes
**

Of course the
Physical material world
Needs attention too
But they are
By nature more obvious
But this too changed

When I saw
What was already mine
My desire for more
Declined greatly

I started to feel
Contentment drift in
Fleetingly here and there
Difficult to keep hold of
Even more difficult
To recognise and own

Before this I had
Never given much thought
To the word 'contentment'
It was so good
To put a name to the feeling
Admitting I had sensed it
Because at first I felt guilty

How could I feel content
When so much
Was wrong in my life
When big parts of me
Were so broken
When I felt so very lonely

But contentment was there to be found

Humility came next
Only when I wasn't looking
By its very nature

My gentle side
Became my strength
I grew in confidence

With Ann's depression
In view for me to see
It helped me to
Stop feeling guilty
For having mine

A guilt I had carried
All of my life
Though not always
Recognised as such
Or even given that name.

**

In front of me
My Sad Light Box
Used each morning
Staving off hopefully
The Autumn blues
With pink geraniums
On my table
Enjoying the light too
**

Quotes
Ann dares us
'To live fully
Right where we are'

'All we have to decide
Is what to do
With the time
That is given to us'
JRR Tolkien

LOVE

The beginning of love

First you receive it
Then you share it
It flows forward
Backwards, blends, melds
Grows, shrinks, stretches

Dependant on others
Until aware enough
Of self and choices
By now the brain is wired

Positive childhood
Equipped with skills
Loved, confident, educated
Ready to make Good choices

Or

A negative beginning
Unprepared for life
Thrown into the world
With little understanding
Bewildered, unloved, unaware
Little or no education
Poor mental health

No wonder life is easier
For some than others
Love can break you
Or make you

We all look for love
But it takes
Sometimes a lifetime
To look for it
In the right places

Connections tight or loose
Different for everyone
You dance together
Searching for the right steps
Stepping on toes
Jumping through hoops
Movement in constant flux

Chemistry like a magnet
Grabs your attention
Bodies filled with desire
Overrides intelligence

Spiritual needs
Get put to one side
But without these
It's to no avail
Wasted, leaving you empty

The need to be seen
Not what you're wearing
Your shape or your size
A smile or a frown, no!

Inside your being
Unseen for most
Awake my sleeping heart
Spirit that never dies
Shapeshifting
Eternal growth
Let me feed you with
Understanding of love
In its many forms

Firstly love thy self
Know your worth
Understand your gifts
Be kind and gentle
TO YOU
True to who you are
Made, uniquely

I lay before you
A banquet of hope
I share joy in the moment
In quietness, find peace
In truth lives reality

Love I have your back
You shine from my eyes
Faith in the future
Open heart of tenderness
Courage to move forward
Gifts handed down
One life at a time

We can live this life
Seeing it's beauty
Marvel at it's complexity
Revere it's magnificence

Worship it's maker
Feeling deep gratitude
For who we are, and
Whom we are to become
All of this
Over the passage of time

Endless time

JOY

Can joy be found I ask myself
If you haven't known sadness
Is it measured by your experience
Of past pain

Can it be lost
If you don't know where
To look for it
Can it be invisible to those
To blind to see

When we feel joy
Do we acknowledge it
Welcome it in
Give it a chair so to speak
Be grateful for it's presence
Ask it to stay
Allowing it to fill us full

Or

When joy does come
Do you see it doesn't need fixing
So you ignore it
And it thinks you don't want it
So it goes on its way
Feeling rejected
So now it's less willing
To knock on your door again

In recent times
I have felt more of my own grief
Also the grief of the world
There is so much sadness
In these human lives

I know so many people
Grieving loss in different ways
It's not just me
We get lost in it

People share their loss
So it gets added to yours
Carrying it around
Is exhausting for all

But there is a different way
A new way for me
I can be present with the grief
On the one hand

Then

On the other hand
Still on the same plane
I can look for the joy
It is often there

We can do them both
Alongside each other
At first I found this surprising!!

This doesn't mean
We are not allowing the sadness
What it does mean
Is we are not wallowing in it
But seeing the joy and beauty too
When you really look
There is so much to see

We are complex beings
Often so caught up
In the spin and whirl of life
We forget to look deep :-(

RAGE

One of the many
Different parts of me
Or should I say
OF ALL OF US

Anger is the most difficult
Of emotions to admit to
I have kept a lid on it
From childhood
Having been taught
Not to show it

BUT

I noticed my partners
Seemed to think
                    It was their right
                    To vent
But as soon as I did
I was stamped on (control)

SO

We are conditioned
As women
Not to show our rage

It is seen as unlady like
We are told people won't
Want to be our friends
If we get mad

This was so ingrained
I lost the ability to express
My hurts, anger, fear
They got driven inside
DEEP INSIDE

Bottled up emotions
Put In kilner like jars
Shoved into storage
Partitioned off in my mind
Stored in my muscle memory
And I know I'm not alone

Is it any wonder
That we go around
With the mists of sadness
Our minds clouded
With the unexpressed
And eventually deadened anger

So many of us have held onto this
For so many years
In many case decades
Nearly a lifetime

Many of us develop
Passive aggressive patterns
Our actions seem soft
But we find new ways
To be in control
Ways that are difficult to define
And hard for us and others
To fathom

Lately I have learned
How to show and express
This anger in more controlled
Ways
With conscious intention
Responding wisely
With heart and mind
Connecting together

Sometimes I fail

I have learned and understood
How important
My anger is
In fact it's actually essential
To my survival

A vital instrument
A radar for injustice
Also a catalyst for change

Rage helps me
Set my boundaries
Showing me my real
POWER is not in my servitude
As I was once taught
However it is in my humility

Anger is my best friend
It helps keep me safe
Enables me to make
Better choices

Teaching girls to be compliant
Makes me so cross
This feels like men taking away
Our voices and choices

It also encourages poor mental health

INNER CHILD

Oh for the heart of a child
Innocent, loving, playful
NEEDY!

Where does fear begin
Is it the first cry
Outside the safety of the womb
Let loose in a dysfunctional world
Arriving with a new mind
Clean and clear
Like a new canvas
Ready to be imprinted
Painted with your parents
Colours and shapes
Habits, sayings, rituals and beliefs

Brokenness passed down the line
From one generation to the next

You don't get to choose
Who your parents will be
It's the luck of the…..draw!

I have never been
A lottery winner…
Not even a raffle ticket
That has never mattered
But I wish I'd had
More luck with my parents

My parents
Had good intentions
They loved me
But fate cast a dark shadow
Over my mother

One of four girls
Living in poverty
Food was very scarce
This took its toll
On all of their physical health

Mother tells this story:

Their great aunt
Had plenty of money and food
Once a week she paid them a visit
Bring the leftover Sunday joint

Most of the time
This was the only meat
They had in a week
Money was so short
Grandad was a shoe mender

My daddy far away in the war
Tucked way up in the Hebrides
Mummy on her own for years
With me in tow
Her mother with poor health

Unknown to mummy
And undetected for decades
She has an under active
Thyroid problem

Years later it was treated
But too late to stop
The breakdowns that
Took over her whole life

This began
With water running
Down the kitchen wall
My mummy goes to pieces
I am 5 years old
From that day on
She was a mess
OCD developed
Overriding everything
Overwhelming for daddy
Devastating for me

It was as if overnight
I lost the lady
I knew as mummy
She being my whole world

In her place
A woman with demands
One I had to please
At all costs
Or I would upset her

It felt like everything I did
My inability to get it right
Made her shaky and sad
I walked on eggshells

I was paralyzed with fear
If I dropped anything
It became dirty

I couldn't touch certain things
Touching and doing
Had to be in the right order
This it seemed was essential
It was all a great mystery to me

It took her hours to dress me
Everything had to be aired
Individually in front of the fire
Before being put on
I would stand there shivering

So long ago

Yet still I can picture it
As it happened

See the electric fire
Her mottled skin
From being too close to it
Poor her, poor daddy
Poor me!

I recall all of this

Because our inner child
Stays with us
Throughout our whole lives
Imprinted from birth

It is difficult to meet
Your own needs
When you haven't been shown
How
Or don't remember
What a good parent does

Over the years
I have been learning
To talk with my inner child
When I can register her needs

I comfort and reassure her
She gets frightened
In unusual ways
She can be very hard work

I recently learned from a friend
To use different cuddly toys
Depending on what Gillian is
Experiencing

I have only just started this

I have a soft reindeer
I am going to use for sadness

A leopard cub
For feelings of rejection

I am going to buy a dragon
For my anger
I have not got any further yet

Gillian or Gill
I am very grateful for her
She is so creative, full of ideas
Playful and so much
Fun to have around
'On a good day'
And the only company I have had
Most of the time in the last 10 years

Many of us are fortunate
We seem to instinctively know how
To bring up our children
But forget to nurture ourselves

I am still learning

POET

It's nearly 4 years
Since I started my new life
One I should've had
All of my life
It's hard to not have regrets
But that's a time waster
I need to make
The most of what's left

In this my new life I am a poet

First time I wrote a poem
Was when I was at school
Probably about 12 years old
"The witches squabble"

Remembering the excitement
And surprise that I could
It was then a school project
Everyone was doing it
So I didn't give it a second thought

Some of the words still float up
From the recesses of my mind
Where memories are filed away
Not all the words are left
They have disappeared over time

The Witches

The witches on their brooms fly high
Into the dark and eerie sky
They screech squabble scowl and scratch
And frighten the birds that have just been hatched

Mothers draw their curtains tight
Till dawn shows it's first glimpse of light
With this the witches disappear
Peace and quiet reigns once more here

This may be
The first time
I've written this since school
60 or so years ago
Did I get it right?

A first poem
I was so pleased
Back then

I wrote a reflective poem at 18
Sat on the top deck
Going who knows where
Called 'when all alone'
Stored in the back of my head

Bits pop up out of the blue
Strange and wonderful
Thought I might
Write it down properly
For the first time
Especially for this book

It's been in there
Over fifty years so here goes

Sat here now
I search for all the verses
They fade in and out
I catch some of them
Write what I've found
Decide to sleep on it
See what happens
When I wake tomorrow

When Alone

When all alone I sit and think
About the days gone by
As I sit my heart does sink
Old age is creeping nigh

My teens came and went
Romance did fill my life
confused and yet content
I soon became a wife

We were blessed with baby twins
A little boy and girl
My heart full to the brim
Our lives in a spinning whirl

My little ones they grow up fast
They were my pride and joy
How long would my happiness last
I so loved my girl and boy

..........................left home
To make their lives elsewhere
....
....

The years drifted on and on
Then one day I did awake
Found my husband dead and gone
My heart did nearly break

I am now at peace with everything
As wise as I will ever be
My lips will always laugh and sing
And I'll keep my memories close to me

There are holes
In this poem
Where once there were words
but I kind of like that
You get to fill in the blanks

As you will read
My dreams in this poem
Don't all go to plan
But I do get my boy and girl
Life is a mystery waiting to happen

If I were to write
The ending to my last few years
This life now!
I wonder what I would write
Would it be as in the poem
What I want to happen
Against
What will probably take place
Best not to know maybe

Love and poems go together

Meeting my ex husband

I put an advert in a newspaper
South Wales Echo
'Intelligent caring Christian lady
                    Middle years seeks
                    Similar gentleman'

Eleven replies
I spoke to a few
They weren't Christian
Not in a real way
Just on the surface

I met a couple
But not right for me
Sent up a prayer
Vicar would be special
Someone trustworthy
Man of God

A soft voiced vicar
Phones me, he says
God looked in his Filofax and said
'I have just the one here with dark curly hair'
What a blessing
Answered prayers

I wrote many love poems
Was so surprised
Just how good I thought they were

My vicar followed
A group of poets
(One was his best friend)
I asked him
Could I read mine out
At one of their sessions

BUT

He said they were 'real poets'...............
I didn't write a poem again
Wish I had kept them

TILL

70th Birthday

Time to party
Asked - 'what would I like'.
By my friend Dru
I think long and hard
I come up with a
'A story teller'

It's also suggested
We could write poems
I had heard some of hers
They were lovely

So 'I guessed I could try'

One day I go out
Looking for inspiration
Ending up down at
Aberthaw power station

I park the car
Go for a meander
Up a road I don't know
What a surprise!

I see a field full
Cow Parsley everywhere
My favourite wildflower

Eyes out on stalks
Heart pounding
With pen and paper
It just happens
Feels like Divine inspiration

An Experience Being Experienced on 20th July 2014

Cow parsley as far as the eye can see
And wow it's nearly as tall as me
Locked gate says 'you must keep out'
But my joy by this sight is too much, I shout

My heart leaps over to photo the lot
The sun is high and I am hot
My spirit soars deep inside of me
A memory for winter I long to see

A reminder to live in the here and now
Makes the experience double fold
Some for now and some for later
Cake and eat it comes to my mind

Oh how we can make so much more of less
This could have been a place just passed
Instead it's restored my spirit and mind
Cost me nothing, just given some time

It's all about what's deep inside, what's hidden
Dig deep I say, feel the world around
See its beauty and listen to its sound
Wind's blowing, all form moves about

Ever changing like we hope to be
Changing from what we are, to whom we can't see
Only God in his wisdom can see ahead
Thank you Lord for the kaleidoscope of life

For changes and challenges, the good and the great
For memories like pearls of wisdom to hold
Let us store them like apples are stored in a draw
Ready for winter and the long dark days

Let's throw out the rotten ones,
Just let them go, it's hard I know, I know
But good food for thought, file them away
They can't be bought it's important to say
You have to experience it all for yourself
Give yourself time to have fun and to play
YOU, no one else, before it's too late
You too can sit at the farmers gate

And be in the here and now, NOW

And then

With some clouds gathering on the circle's edge
Others drift just hanging loose
A feeling of freedom as they float by
I am free this minute, I have nowhere to be

And as I move away from this farmers gate
A swift flies his wings in a figure of eight
The fields all around are full of life
The beauty overflows I'm on the edge of a knife

Sharp focus the power station is so close by
Yet it's I, who have the real power to live or die
You see, I have a walking friend called God
You will glimpse him if I have got it right

A fly lands on my hand for a wash
It would be so easy to kill him - squash
But I'm in a great place in my mind
So I let him live, power of a kind, to be kind.

Just the one poem
I think it's a fluke
One of those moments

When I look back
I can see there have been
A number of these moments

My party date arrives
Family and friends gather
Special afternoon tea
With a birthday cake
Just for me

The storyteller performs
She is a lovely lady

I read out my poem
With deep feeling
A premier performance
For ME
To great adulation

I didn't see
This was the real me
My future to come
A performance poet

Since joining
Llantwit Writing Circle
It's nearly four years
Seeing I can write

Releasing my thoughts
I start to think poetry
Read poetry books
Love some hate others
Gives me understanding
Of how diverse it can be

It feels I am opening
The recesses of my mind
Tapping into
Unexplored territory

I can feel my mind
Changing
It's like magic

As if words float
Though the air
And my mind catches them
At strange unconnected times
From the ethers just passing by

On their way
To whoever is open
To receive them that day

Verse pours out
I grab bits of paper
Speak it into my phone
Anything that is handy

I CATCH IT

Otherwise it's just gone
And it doesn't hang about

Lost forever
Or
Gone to the next
Receptive person

These are only
Meanderings :-))

Recently I have collected
10 poems in as many days

Then nothing

I think I have
Lost the ability
Can't find a single phrase
I feel bewildered

Then out of the blue
When I'm not looking
It starts again

So exciting
I love words
When used wisely

I struggle
When people just blab
Saying nothing
Talking for the sake of it
Or constantly complaining

Such a waste
Waste of words
Waste of listening
Waste of time

With so many words
All mixed up
We get to miss
The important ones

Sifting through them
Looking for what's
Being conveyed
They lose their immediacy
Their value

God spoke everything into being
And he was precise

FESTIVALS

Here in Llantwit Major
July 2021
We had a mini festival

The festival was called
These Three Streams
Literature, music and art

All held in our
Ancient and beautiful
St Illtud's church
Originating from
Foundations
Going back to 500 AD

My part in this
To put on an art exhibition

Turned out to be
A backdrop to the happenings
It was a lot of work
Months of preparing
Getting all my work
Ready for display

Being a backdrop
Didn't give me any sales
Or appreciation

I wrote 2 poems
Especially for the festival
I opened and closed
The open mike event
Which was held in the evening

I so enjoy performing
I always wear a hat
I now have about 20
I wear a different one
For each poem

I have always loved hats
So having a reason
To wear them
Is a real thrill for me

I had lots of people
Come and thank me
For my poems
Saying they had
Touched them on a
Deeper level and in different ways

This Holy Place

As I enter this space a musty smell of centuries
Fills me with memories of many churches past
My mind goes to incense and the bouquet of flowers
I smell fresh coffee and oh yes home-made cakes
All part of life in this Holy place

I hear distant echoes of years gone by
Ancient walls clinging to whispered prayers
Bells ringing, singing, chants and alleluias
Deep anguished sobbing broken by laughter
A Cacophony of sound in this Holy place

I see light streaming through pictured windows
Candles lit to remember great grandmas and uncles
Stones in loving memory of who came before
Crosses, sacred altars, pulpits, plaques, sculptures
All sacred parts of this holy place

Spirit like breezes brushing your face
Sense His presence guiding and feeding
Filling us with joy peace and the greatest, His love
Going before and behind, protecting us all
And that's not just in this Holy place

Flowers in bunches and blossom on trees
Poses on graves some plastic, nasty but modern
The old and the new entwined altogether
Some you will like and some that you won't
The centuries roll on and on, in this Holy place

Curtsy and bow and the sign of the cross
Royal robes given to all who believe
Towers and rafters and old stones galore
Tradition, repetition, ritual bread and wine
Feast and famine all known in this Holy place

I see children dancing among the gravestones
Ancient and modern like the old hymnbook
Life mingling with death in harmony
A continuing line of natural progression
Changing, yet always the same in this Holy place

At the end of the day we will see, that it isn't
The building, that makes this holy place
It's people, like you and me, everyone
Without us it would be just an 'old building'
10,000 people and more made this Holy place.

Be still and listen to your own heart beating
Make the most of your turn here on earth
Leave behind you, something good to remember
Love lasts the test of time when passed on
You'll find plenty of that in this Holy place

All this in the presence of the Lord of the universe
Father God, Jesus the son and Spirit of Holiness
The three in one past and present and future
Royal purple and gold and red blood, shed for us
All come together in this holy place

2022 the festival
Grows exponentially
Held over three days
At many different venues

There were lots of
Lovely workshops
Talks and demonstrations
The worldwide group
Urban Sketchers met

A poet's evening
With street food

I get to be part
Of a treasure hunt
With two of my paintings
One made especially

It's in celebration
Of this festival
This took me 60 hrs
To paint in mixed media
The theme taken from
William Shakespeare's
Twelfth Night

The second painting
A renovated picture
One of my first
When arriving here

My third painting
A smaller one
Placed in a shop
Opened as a gallery
Just for the festival
It sold

This all culminated
In an evening
Of celebration
'Pints and Poems'
Was born
Now chartered
Once a month
In the local White Hart

I so love a big audience
Enjoyed my night immensely
Even the comments
'That was a bit near the mark'
From people not knowing
It was written
Because of my Ex
And his appalling behaviour

All Balls

I was like a rubber ball that
Kept bouncing back to you
But now this ball is out of touch
Not playing this unfair game
You broke all the rules of love
And left me for almost dead

For me it takes a lot of balls
To describe my time with you
The constant play between us
I'd say 'you are just playing'
You'd say 'yes and I am good'
What a sad admittance that is

No good at true life you lie
Goalie and player all in one
15 years without understanding
I played the game in ignorance
Unaware it was even a game gave
My heart thinking yours was true

Balls, one for every personality
Soft ball playful gentle fun-ish
I hold you close and love you dearly
You hold me too and call me Gorgeous
Arrange our holidays keep things orderly
Make me feel safe protected loved

Table tennis ball is me I think
Can be strong delicate so tap me
Back and forth, if you miss me
I will also bounce well on the floor
Easy going visually pleasing light free
Ping pong gentle, loving and giving

Beach ball good away on holidays
Steady rhythm each day chilled
Not much excitement, needs to
'keep me calm' that's what he says
I say 'controlled' though not back then
Lots of hot wind I should pull out the plug

Football big bombastic sadistic fellow
All puffed up with arrogance and pride
Having the answers to everything
Stamping feet hard as you walk by
Thumping up the stairs across landing
What do you do with footballs - kick them hard

Tennis balls I like the least of all
Come from nowhere fast and very hard
Served up over and over again
Insist it's in, when I know it's out
Criticizes me for getting it all wrong
This ball I hit against a brick wall

Over and over I hit as hard as I can
I feel I can never hit hard enough
I want to hear it scream and shout
Beg me to stop as I often begged you
Like you I refuse to listen or stop
Want to break you to pieces… slowly

The golf ball the hardest of them all
You can swing at it with mighty strokes
But mostly you miss, like you it just sits
Nothing penetrates it's hard outer core
Inside it's as tight as it's possible to be
It won't move it's position no matter what

So what does one do with a hard ball
That won't play the game as it should
Hit it so hard it gets lost in the rough
Hopefully never to be seen again
Or put it into a black watery hole
And leave there to rot for millennia and more
Lottery balls we did not actually need
We had my house it seemed instead
Manipulated every penny spent on him
Debts occurred despite all of this
Never satisfied always wanting more
More of something anything will do - especially bikes

I think how great my need was for you
When actually it was you needed me
To play out your games your so needy
'Ha ha ha', I know you would say
'You know me Gill', 'Yes, it's a shame you don't'
'I am an island' but not when alone

I would so love to be his terrier
And turn on him as he did on me
No matter what he said or tried to do
Not letting him out of that corner
Twisting his mind till he went mad
Locking him up in a self made prison

Oh actually
That's where he already is!
Oubliette - meaning dungeon and forgiveness (I hope that follows)

PS

I left behind me an unexplored bomb
This is definitely not for the bathtub
A bomb that is forever unstable
Apparently impossible to deactivate
One determined to get his own way
Because 'I am the only important PERSON'

PPS

This ping ball is no longer being hit
I am free to be exactly who I am
A hard lesson I was taught by you
Strangely it was one I needed to know
You can never solely rely on anyone
It's all within you hidden ready to find

This very week
I have written
My one hundredth poem

I need to celebrate

I will announce it
In my writing circle
And perform it

I say one hundred
It could be more than….
I'm just guessing here
It doesn't sound very much
But when you
Really think about it!!

That's a minimum of two thousand
Five hundred lines
Of verse AT LEAST
And remember
I am just the do everyone's
Maths homework girl

Picture perfect
Forever Friends

Painted friends sit talking on my wall
Family photos join the conversation
They see each other every single day
So there's often, not very much to say
We know each other's history well
Go back in memory for many years

Milk spills, but there's no cat to lick
Cake growing stale but we can't eat
Where has our maker gone to now
We haven't seen her here for days
She generously feeds us with her life
Without her, there simply is no tale

Then one day she comes storming in
Boots full of snow and dripping face
Jumps up and down says how good
Seeing familiar faces is once more
Life for us begins again, a new story
She has found a friend that's alive, real

Not one she's made 'like all of us'
Here's my gift, she says we can share
He's so full of love, passion - male
We've not seen man much before this
She spends the day with smiley face
Showing us off, introducing him

This of course, is all in her mind
What she wants to happen, we see
We play along with her, it's such fun
Though we sense it will end in tears
Having watched her on the dating sites
Her hopes high, then dashed again

We love her dearly, are part of her
She birthed us from a blank page
Gave us the life we have right now
We want to help her, pay her back
Just where to start, we have no clue
Though always there come rain or shine

She will go before we do
Loyal to the end forever friends

Writing a poem
Is just the beginning
Of a lengthy process

Next they need editing
But not so much
That they loose
Their freshness and spontaneity
The immediacy of the flow
Needs to stay

For me printing is next
If I can't see it
In black and white
I'm frightened it will get lost
In the ethers of the net

Once printed
At least it's safe

Next it gets filed

Now for a second edit
Then proofreading
My granddaughter Megan's
In charge here

Over time
She has learned
To help with editing too

Her mind so keen
She has connected
To my way of thinking

She can come up
With just the right
Replacements needed
Often when I seem unable
She is my little miracle

Megan also works out
The rhythms
When I have been
Too artistic or slap dash
She helps me keep it tight
When I need to

This is so wonderful
I don't know whether
She really understands
Just what a gift
She is to me

We feel our way
We know we need
A system
That works for us
We need to know
What stage
Each poem is at

The challenge
Was eventually
Understood and met

We tried a number
Of different ways
Laughed a lot in the process😊

We cheered when
At last we got it right
And found it fit for purpose

We still have
Much to do
But the whole process
Has been
As much about
Friendship and sharing
As it has been
About producing
A poetry book
That will hopefully
Encourage people
In their day to day lives

I am a thinker
There is nothing
New in this

I have always
Processed on a deep level
And often rehearsed
In my mind over and over
How my thoughts were wasted
Never used productively

So now

The writing of my poetry
Followed by this free verse book
Gives me an opportunity
To reveal
The inner workings
Of my mind
I get to recycle my thoughts
Sharing and hopefully
Enlightening others

For me

There is nothing more exciting
Than understanding
How another mind works
On a subconscious level

This is why I was born
It all makes sense
Of this my challenging life

Born to write maybe

But found accidentally
A causal invitation
To join a new writing circle

I'd thought
My broken life had got in the way
But without it
I could never
NEVER
Have understood so much

My writing would
Have been shallow
Devoid of depth and understanding
My pain was needed
To write the way I do

That is a real revelation
Only being revealed
As I write this here and now

WOW!!

PANDEMIC 2019

It starts in Wuhan City
Hubei Province, China
December

At first
Like everyone else
I think it's too far away to affect me

I feel horrified
Watching them on TV
Dragging people out
From their homes
Kicking and shrieking
I felt panic for them
I am an empath
I was thunderstruck

I wondered just how
They knew who
And where these people
These particular people
Lived and why
They were so dangerous

I feel safe
Where I am
But not for long

With a flash of light
Suddenly I realise
It's coming here
So
Stock up with food

It's January now

Strange what I choose
Cornflour, Bisto, flour
Dried milk, mounds of it
Much goes out of date
Custard powder
3 salad creams
2 Daddies sauces
Tinned fruit
Even 18 toilet rolls
Though to be honest
They were a lucky gift
Before there was any
Hint of this tragedy

My freezers full

**

In the sides
Of my sash windows
Every winter
Hundreds of ladybirds
Hibernate huddled together
I think at least they are safe
Wishing I was them
**

Life is still going on
Much the same
People going about
Their lives not realising
How near the virus was
Not knowing It would change
All our lives

Day by day
I feel more and more
Fearful for the world

Later in March

I watch the news
Empty shelves
Particularly toilet paper
What's the panic
As children we used
Old newspapers

But I can say that
I have an unexpected stash

I start to write a journal
Every single day
This was three fold

Firstly for my mental health

Secondly as a gift
For my granddaughter
When I am gone
She will have this
A reminder of me
Love and laughter
Shared over the years

Thirdly it was sent to
Swansea University
See Facebook below

I have picked 3 examples

March 22nd Wednesday 2020

It's Mothering Sunday, my mother has been dead for 35 years, as strange as it may sound I feel I know her more now than I ever did when she was alive. Finding out more about my father when he dictates his story to me, must be 3 years ago now, I was given a real insight into their relationship. He was quite a mild man but he had a temper easily sprung and she was sensitive. It was wartime and they lived in Birmingham where 1,852 tons of bombs were dropped. He was posted to Scotland, she was pregnant and gave birth to me on her own. I can really empathise with her as I sit here on Mother's Day in a war like (pandemic) situation. As the years pass I feel more and more love for the mother I saw little of due to her mental health, and today send her my love with so much more understanding, God bless you mum xxx

The government asked people not to visit their mothers today, due to the Coronavirus :-(

April 3rd Friday 2020

I am feeling really lonely today. There is so much to see and hear in the countryside, but life is always so much better if there is someone with you. Living alone so no one to share my days, my thoughts, my ups and downs. I know there are so many other people out there in the same position and it's tough, really tough.

I am so glad I have my journal, but yesterday I couldn't write I felt the well of my creativity had just dried up, I was spent nothing left to write:-(

Today is another day, life goes on and I feel a poem coming on, this is a good sign and I have just the first line so far 'I look for you the one my heart always knew I'd find' I wonder where that is going to lead me to.

I pick a single celandine, it's beautiful but it has lost it's glory on it's own! I put it in the brook and watch as it speeds away, lost to me the earth and the sun. Lost like a lot of us feel right now! I hear a child in the background howling, I let her cry be my cry too. When we are children we can allow our feelings to show, as adults we keep them close to our chests we don't want to be seen as week. We all have strength inside of us, we need to dig deep to find it, sometimes I will and others times I won't and that's okay, as long as I pick myself up at the end of it, brush myself off and start over again.

May 27th Wednesday 2020

Well I don't believe what I've just seen, a red damselfly came and sat on my knee. The most beautiful deep red colour with such a slender body, large red eyes and long lace like wings I wanted to freeze time. What a lovely thing to happen! I'm sat in my usual place in the Body park having just been for my walk. It's concious moments like this that last if you look at the detail and feel the joy. I might not always be able to remember what day it is in this pandemic, but I will always recall the day the damselfly landed on my knee, a mindful moment for my memory box.

A strange time for me having written this journal for 3 months, talked to you through this pandemic and now it's time to say goodbye, it feels so final, I guess I could write another one!

I want to sing 'we'll meet again' but I have run out of room on my last page of this beautiful material covered journal, and my writing is having to get smaller and:-)(

All my poems
Written during this time.
A period of 3 months
Then a few more
Random entries I think
Went as well
Along with my paintings

These my contributions
Giving understanding
History in the making
Connecting the generations
Creating a clearer picture
Of the present from the past
How it came about
So more confidence
For the future……Hopefully

A good process for me
Knowing I was sharing
With a world
That for the present
I couldn't be a part of
Gave me a purpose
Those long weeks

All is Love

I go up a high tower in my mind
Closer to the sky the air is sweet
And as I peer all around me now
I see hints of spring here and there
White of daisy, yellow celandine
Bits of blue forget-me-not

If I were to die in all of this
Or you or someone else that's close
Let us remember them with love
The life they lived, the good in them
But while we live, let's really love
And love some more for love is all

Wrapped in Safety

I wrap myself in jammies and a quilt
Curl up in bed and close my eyes
I sigh a sigh, relief I'm safe for now
Leaving the hand washing and soap behind
I can touch all that I can feel from here
Fear drifts off as I now feel safe

I close my eyes and remember better times
When I could hug, shake hands, kiss cheeks
Stand so close I could feel life's breath
Laugh without worry of spreading germs
But today I notice from a distant smile
The postman with the sparkling eyes

The vision stays!

This turned into 4 months
Seeing only
My daughter and granddaughter
From a distance
As they delivered my shopping
At the far end of a bridge
Outside of my duplex

I am so inward looking
By now
When I see them
It's as if I am watching
From reversed binoculars

They seem unreal
Small dots in the distance
Similar to a live show
Say at Wembley stadium
Untouchable moving puppets

I want to hug them
Too frightened to cwtch
My own children
My daughter a key worker

My umbrella is nowhere
To be seen
I can't hide from
What feels like
Constant storms

No dancing
In between the raindrops
Sadly for me and others
Raindrops keep falling
From our eyes

So much pain
People dying in droves
It's difficult to know
Where to store
All the bodies

Homes for the elderly
Losing so many people
Because of lack
Of protective clothing
Masks in particular

THE WORLD'S IN CRISIS

ZOOM

So this is life
What can I do
To make a difference
In this broken world

Probably about 6 months
Before this pandemic
I joined a small group
Called cwtch

A welsh word for hug

I go along fortnightly
Share a meditation
Talk about healthy eating
Introduce new tools
For emotional support

Also

I join Bro radio
Training to broadcast
And find local news
I was excited by this

Like everything else
This was halted
By this terrible CoronaVirus

Weeks go by

A new wind blows💨

GVS a charity
Umbrella for cwtch
Asked if I would
Run classes on zoom
As a volunteer

We called them
"Time for you"
Every week for 9 months
I prepared and shared
2 hour courses

Always encouraging
Good mental health practises
Scattered amongst
Words, crafts and art
Something new each time
It was a real challenge

We looked at many
Emotional tools
When and how
They could be best used

I'll name just a few

We made worry dolls
The idea came
Originally from Spain
We tell the dolls
Our worries and leave these
With them under our pillows
While we sleep in more peace

Then

Greek worry beads
From ancient times
Made in our own designs
I remembered seeing them
When I was in Greece

Older people sitting around
With them in their hands
They were black
Ours brightly coloured

And

We read pieces from books
One I remember well
The Boy, the Mole and the Fox
So very thought provoking
Softening our minds
Thinking of friendships
                    kindness and love

Next

We moved on to artists
Sourced from YouTube
I choose abstract painters
So all abilities could have a go

Janet Skates
Really inspired us

After one of the sessions
From another artist
Can't remember her name
My painting
(I always did a demo)
Looked particularly
Different and interesting
I turned it into

'Garden of remembrance'
Acrylic and collage
I sold this one
So painted another similar

GVS made prints
Full size and cards
We sold them for charity

It was at this time
I invented emotional socks
Red for anger
Black for sadness
Orange for joy
Stripes for fear

We discovered from this
How little attention we give
To the joy we feel
As it doesn't ask to be fixed

But JOY
Is so important
We need to recognise
The positives in life
In so doing lift our moods
And find yes! Gratitude again

We started
Talking to them all
Having a conversation
As puppets on our hands
Asking each one
Where have you been today
Anger
Joy
Fear
Sadness
Then waiting for the answers

This enables you to get
An understanding
Of your deeper self
Helps you process your day
Particularly good for those
Of us living on our own
'Someone to talk to'

Each session
We end with
A meditation
I bought a book
Full of meditations
But they were patented
So I used them as
Inspirations for my own meditations

In the process
I started to record them
As the group said
They wanted my voice
To listen to at home

All this gave me a focus
And a purpose
The group ended
Just before Christmas 2020
I wrote them a poem

Cwtch me when

It's been so long

Cwtch a year old, it's Happy Birthday
Who would have thought this name
Would be the very thing we couldn't do
The most yearned and longed for of all
Touch me only on your iPad they say
Keep 2 meters away no matter what

This was the agony for most people
16 weeks without being hugged at all
Isolation, pain, desperation that's sharp
Stiff upper lip was hard to keep to
Brave face with a smile on your lips
But in our hearts we are all crying

Touch the most precious of life's gifts
As chemicals from two beings merge
Making something new that feels so good
When we don't get touched we lose
The connection that's so important
It makes us feel whole and very loved

Cwtch me when
One day soon I hope

FACEBOOK

On my page
It showed an advert
From Swansea university
They were looking for journalists
Poets and artists

They were making an archive
Of people's lives
In this pandemic
In the same way
They had done
Post Second World War

I couldn't resist
Becoming part of history

For four months
Everyday
One after another
After another
I wrote my journal

At first I write
Directly into the journal
A beautiful book
Covered in green Chinese material
It seemed appropriate
In more ways than one

Eventually as I learn
More technology
I speak into my phone
Using Note's
Then airdropping it
On to my iPad

**
I am so please with myself
Fancy me being able
To perform this kind of magic
Every time I do it I am in awe
Surprised as I watch it work
Every time!!
It is so easy peasy
**

Once it's on my iPad
I edit it
Now I copy it
Into my journal
By hand it's a
Long process
But I keep at it
Remembering why I am doing it

Poetry poured out of me
Riding on the high seas
Of all the emotions
The full spectrum
A poets dream
In a real awake nightmare

All of my work
During this time
Was sent monthly
To Swansea University

Mike from the university
Has said there might
One day in the future
Be a book of all the entries
More than a hundred
People took part
To varying degrees

All this helped me to stay
Focused
On life here and now
Getting through each day
One baby step at a time

PANDEMIC YouTube

Every night I attended
The university of YouTube
I sat upstairs
In the same easy chair

It became a repeated ritual
I looked forward to it
Felt very excited as I hungrily
Scoured the internet

Like a ravenous lion
I'm ready to devour
Whatever I'm fed

But

Always art of some kind
Kind being the operative word
So many artists
Sharing their knowledge

I explored the many mediums
Ideas on form and content
How to make more of colours
What to buy, just not where
But that fell into place

It started to feel
Like YouTube had
Control over me
With no effort
As the moon over the earth
I was hooked
A willing student

Not content to just watch
I had to experiment
With each day's meal
Gradually becoming
An even more accomplished artist
I grew so much this year
Like I was learning

All the things
Discovering all the gifts
I should have learnt
My entire life
My neuropaths opening
Absorption on overload

So I am watching art
Doing art
Journaling
Writing poetry
Now writing this book

I got to a place
Where I could see
I needed to follow
Only one road at a time

So at this moment
I have my writing head on
Longing to paint

It's been 5 months
But then I would
Need to stop writing
This stops my brain
Imploding and keeps me sane

WRITING CIRCLE

June pre pandemic
Hard to remember
Life as it was back then
Better in general
But looking back
I see how I have grown
Much happier now

So why?

I Was invited
By an acquaintance Kath
Who has since
Become a good friend
To join her writing group
It became The Writing Circle
30 people on opening night
At least, in one tiny room
Chaotic but fun

Gradually ……..
It whittles down to a core of 10

The second meeting we're
Given a writing prompt
It's so much fun
We get to share our writing
Listening to each other

As I am writing mine
I think it will be rubbish

To my surprise
Phil the writer (of 84 books))
Says he's amazed
How I wrote all that
In the time we had
I remember it as ten minutes

It was well received
I have a very big smile on my face :-))
So here it is

Old Bag

I found this old bag
In my attic one day
Why this one when
There are at least
10 others, I don't know!

In it was a £10 note
Out of date now, no
Longer legal, then a
List of things to do,
I smile as I read
Things on this list, that
I still haven't done

Nothing really changes,
Patterns carry on through

Paper hanky with tears
From my father's funeral
Only thing I have left
From that day, he 100
Yet what did he leave me
Fear and bottle of Head
And Shoulders shampoo

A thimble, I can't think
Why! A hatpin makes
Me feel safe, now that
I live alone. Earplugs
From a festival and
The constant noise that
Bellowed out. A girl
She can't go anywhere
Without her lipstick!

A spoon, I find hunger
Pangs are warded off
With food I can eat
An old sticky sweet
Just in case I get that
Dry throat, I have
These everywhere you look

Gloves, cold hands warm heart!

So full of stories
This old bag

Well I haven't looked back
Found my muse
Gained confidence
Become curious
To see what I was capable of
The group stretches
Sometimes it shrinks
All a bit elastic
But the core stays
We become close
Open to each other
Listening encouraging
Gradually able
To critique for real

Now just over four years
I haven't missed
Not even one, single meeting
There weren't any in the pandemic:-(

We are all so different
5 have published works
Many are writing fiction
Couple historical factual
With literary license
Two write from real life
Poetry so beautiful

I've written many poems
In this time
A few short stories
Now I am writing
This free verse book

Filled with gratitude
For the gifts I have been given
Sharing my mind

Using these gifts
For my life's purpose

My legacy to all who follow
Showing the road much travelled

This beautiful passage
So full of lessons
Pleasure and pain

So many choices
Difficult decisions
Not easy without the right tools
But I'm a hunter gatherer
My tool box
Gets fuller by the year

My Toolbox

It's not full of nails, hooks or tacks
No screwdrivers, hammers or string
Heavy it's not nor rattles about
Nor mostly used by a man
In some helmet or cap

But it can dig you out of a hole
And lay a smooth path where you go
If climbing the wall it will help you to stop!
And can lighten your load as you go, how?
It's all about finding the right tool for the job

I call it my toolbox I have one at home
And I encourage other people to get their own!
What does it look like I hear you ask?
Well its big, in your face so to speak
A constant reminder to see at a glance

Shall we take a quick look and see inside?
I know! It's empty there's nothing to see
What used to be there, is no more
It's now pinned to my kitchen wall, So!
Much easier to see and to use

It's a list of my emotional tools

Joining this group
One of my better choices
I think back
There's been so many
Wrong turnings
Mistaken junctions
Distractions
Red traffic lights ignored

We meet monthly at first
Gradually our enthusiasm grows
We start to meet fortnightly
It works so much better

The crown in my life
It encourages me to write
As a group we are
Growing each other

Once a month
We have a workshop
Mostly given by one of us
With us all having
Different talents
This works extremely well

We then have
Two weeks to write
Either something
From the workshop
Or
Whatever we are working on

The next meeting
We each take it in turns
To share our words
It is so interesting
To hear our different styles
How we each see the world

We have had many workshops
So I will mention just a few

Historical fiction

Telling the story
Of a particular picture

Writing musical lyrics

Emotional writing

Nonsensical prose or verse

Flash fiction
We were given words
As prompts
Chose a sweet from a box, mine was a Galaxy
This had to be included
Then asked to write a brief piece
No more than 30 words

My words from prompts

Straight	Fire	Sticky	Joyful	Bit	Mindfulness
Eye	Crackle	Sweet	Happy	Suck	Process
Candy	Pop	Stale	Chilled	Chew	Seeing
Hot	Stars	Hard			
Full	Shiny	Wrinkly			
Pink	Far off	Smooth			

From this I wrote the following:

Straight eye candy, hot full lipped in pink, happy hearing the fire pop, crackle, as she sucked her sticky sweet under the galaxy of stars, they seemed so far off while meditating mindfully.

We had 5 minutes
I didn't quite keep to thirty □

All our workshops
Have been inspiring

Festival - These Three Streams

The festival flows
From this Writing Circle
Started by Kath our leader
A small seed planted
In her from the universe perhaps
In fertile soil it grows
And a festival is born
Giving birth is hard work

Kath a lady so full of vitality
Poured her life's energy
Her talent and organizational skills
Gave it all she had
Her vision became a reality
It grow from a half day
To three days and still blossoms

Already the plans
For next year
Sown like bulbs
In the winter
Will be ready to flower
In June once more

Christmas Party 2021

I can't leave out
Our Christmas party
We came in fancy dress
Sarah and I
Came as wild cats
It had to be characters
From a book
Mine was
'The Snow Leopards'

For fun

We had picture prompts
When your turn came you
Picked up a picture
And carried on
With the story
It was surprising
How hard we found this
Considering we are writers

But we laughed a lot
Had a meal
And Seb played his guitar
Beautifully and we all sang
It was very special……magical

Christmas Party 2022

This year
We were really excited
We remembered last year

Again we came in fancy dress
I went as 'The Queen of Hearts'
From 'The Adventures of
Alice in Wonderland'

We were all to go with
A ghost story or a poem
About or why we had chosen
Our fancy dress character

I had written a poem
Which I performed
Laura filmed it on my phone
I so wish I could put
The film in here
But you have the poem instead

At the end where
I say off with his head
I produced a real ax
Made a few people jump

I had cut an apple in quarters
Cut it's top off
Scooped out the middle
Filled it with tomato sauce
And put it back together
When I brought down the ax
Tomato sauce sprayed EVERYWHERE

So

I was kind and gentle
Tender caring and truthful
With hope for my future
And a heart, full of love

So I joined

Yes, I'm a dating site goer
Seems, you can't get much lower
The whole thing is so,so sad
I'm constantly challenged and Mad

So again and again

Another man's not playing fair
Seems he just, doesn't care
Wants it all his own way
But, I'm not going to play!

So now

Let me tell you my dear
Today, I'm in charge here
I've appointed myself Queen
Because I'm not, a has-been

So mean

I am judge and I'm jury
So get used to my fury
This queen of hearts said
Guess? It's off with his head

So!!

We shrieked with laughter

The food was great
The waitresses so helpful
With smiley faces and
Nothing too much trouble
Thank you girls

Everyone else had
Ghost stories
We listened intrigued
They were spooky!!

I love my Writing Circle friends

FRIENDSHIPS

I am truly blessed
With special friends
When I arrived here
A decade ago
I was met with such kindness

Firstly by my daughter
Her husband
And my young granddaughter
All cared for me tenderly
Filled me with their love
I was hard work so broken

What a challenge
Scary to have your mother
So ill living with you
I was so grateful to them
And still am
I felt and was safe
After being SO unsafe

Slowly, painfully slowly
The long journey to recovery
Started one baby step at a time

Family is so important
They love you warts and all
My daughter is a now
A very dear friend
My granddaughter a bright
Light
My son in law has at last
Accepted me
My son who first rescued me
I love dearly too
He is also my friend
We are all friends forever
Forever friends

My friend of 30 years
Shared her space
When I was at my lowest
Hardly able to speak
Or listen for any length
Of time
I would just sit
Accepted respected and loved

Then two people I barely knew
Invited me to stay a while
Six months in the end
I was mothered so beautifully
It felt so wonderful

Tea and a kettle in my room
A hot water bottle in my bed
Flowers by my bedside
Shoulder massages
What more could a girl want

We have become close friends
A very special part of my life
However I turn up
I am loved and heard
WHAT A GIFT

Over the last ten years
I have made some
Lovely friendships
Through my portrait classes
My volunteer work
Art groups and classes
My writing circle
Personal growth groups
Meetings in shops

Connecting with different
Parts of me
Choosing my friends carefully
In this part of my life
Having the confidence
These days to go after
People that meet my needs
Hoping that I return the compliment

What is life about
For me it's about sharing
The journey
Caring for others
In the way you want to be
Cared for

Having each other's backs
Being open hearted
Living in truth
This being the only reality

Connection connection connection
It is our appreciation
Of and for one another
That seals that connection
Recognising where we each are
At any given time
Then connecting at that level

Being humble a new challenge
Going out into the world
With love in your heart
Being kind and gentle
No matter who you meet

Guess what

Another new book

I have just started reading
'Whole Brain Living'
By Jill Bolte Taylor

She is teaching me
All about the different parts
Of my brain

Telling me I can get to know
These four parts
That form who I am
And with understanding
Choose which part
I inhabit at any one time

She explains what each part
Is responsible for
And asks me to find
A name that works for me

I have called No. 1
Wilf coming from self will
He is an elephant
As this part never forgets

No. 2 piglet
My emotional broken child
Who keeps us safe
Our job to reassure and comfort her

No. 3 Peter Rabbit
Joy in the moment
The artist in me
Adrenaline junkie

No. 4 Aslan
The spiritual presence
Sees the bigger picture
Wise and is love

This is my next journey
I feel excited
Ready to move forward
Into the great unknown

Will I meet you there?

AUTHOR'S BIOGRAPHY

As bitter battles rage around the world Olive has her own. For many days now she has been in labour; on her own and frightened, her contractions so painful. It's August, and the heat isn't helping. I seem in no hurry to come into this warring world of 1,800 tons of bombs landing around my birthplace, Birmingham. 'Why isn't Norman Here' she yells at the height of a contraction. Deep down she knows he is in the Hebrides, but at this moment she is delirious.

Eventually I fill my mother's birthing ring of fire, and slip into the pool of blood and morning sunshine. Fists tightly clenched, virgin lungs filling with life's force, my first cries are a welcome sound. Olive has my name ready, Gillian, meaning youthful, unassuming, artistic and silly in a good way, it feels I grew into this name, well chosen for me. 'A Saturday's child works hard for a living'.....oh well here goes.....there are many ways in which to work hard. Mine is to overcome the trauma of my young life and find new and interesting ways to deal with anxiety, which has coloured my whole life many shades of grey and blue, and on a good day bright orange.

Part of my life's work has been to gain understanding of the mind's many aspects and put together an emotional toolbox to heal myself and share with others. Along side this, a life time of reading self help books.

Now a passionate poet and performer full of inspired thinking. Words are so powerful they make music in your mind: dancing into corners, bringing beauty out of shadows, connecting past, present and future giving understanding. Watch as magic does it's healing.

A story teller, author, narrative artist and colourist using many different mediums. I love to play, and get very excited when I see my artist's head working it's wonders. Also a journalist, meditator and seeker of wisdom and Spirit, I have found many sapphires hidden, buried deep for so long, now in the open, bright and sparkling.

Part of my hero's journey has been to stop looking for love in the wrong places. A few abusive husbands later I see I can rely on myself. I have had insightful counsellors over the years helping me, for which I am very grateful. At last I am learning to love myself like the book says 'as if my life depends on it'. Now living on my own with the occasional fruit-fly for company, family just down the road, and in a beautiful creative community on the Welsh coast I am content.

Look out for my next books, pamphlets of poems the first called 'Sea of Consciousness' then 'Nutcracker.....Sweet' followed by non fiction short stories. Enjoy!

Printed in Great Britain
by Amazon

40977644R00128